501 Motor

Other books in the same series

1001 Supersavers
501 Cook's Tips
501 DIY Supersavers
501 Gardening Tips
501 Ways to Save Money

501 Motoring Tips

Money-saving advice for buying and running a car

Tony Bosworth

PIATKUS

First published in 1993 by
Judy Piatkus (Publishers) Ltd of
5 Windmill Street, London W1P 1HF

A catalogue record for this book is
available from the British Library

ISBN 0-7499-1287-1

Edited by Esther Jagger
Cartoons by Ron McTrusty

Set in Linotron Times by
Computerset Ltd, Harmondsworth, Heathrow
Printed and bound in Great Britain by
Mackays of Chatham PLC

Buying a car is usually your single biggest purchase after your home, but for many people the car often ends up being more troublesome and more costly to run! But that need not be the case. This book shows you how to save money right from the start with a series of hints and tips which will help you buy the best car for your needs, at the best possible price.

And once you've got the car of your dreams – new or secondhand – you can learn from this book how to keep it in peak condition, how to save money on running costs, how to be safe on the roads, how to avoid other drivers out there, and, at the end of the day, how to sell your car for the best possible price. *501 Motoring Tips* is all about making your driving enjoyable without costing you your life savings, or your life. Happy motoring!

Tony Bosworth
July 1993

Choosing Your Perfect Car

1 If you are buying a new car, cut down on confusion by following this simple method. First, choose from hatchback, saloon, estate car, sports car, four wheel drive vehicle or people carrier. Next, decide if you ideally want two, three, four or five doors. Then narrow the choice down to two or three individual models of car.

Choosing a Car That Will Keep Its Value

2 Look for a car with high specifications, because such extras ensure a high value when you come to sell. An electric sunroof, electric windows, electric door mirrors, air conditioning, alloy wheels, power steering and central locking – the more the better.

3 Colour has a major effect on the resale value of your car. Avoid dark, boring colours and most definitely avoid beige, which is viewed by the motor trade as the least attractive. So pick a strong colour – solid red is a good choice. Best of all are metallic paint finishes. *See also 19.*

Petrol or Diesel?

Diesel cars are growing in popularity across Europe thanks to their fuel-saving nature. But is a diesel car really a better buy than a petrol-engined car?

4 Buy a diesel-engined car and you can expect the engine to last considerably longer than a petrol one. A diesel can last for around 200,000 miles (322,000 km) while a petrol engine rarely goes beyond 150,000 miles (242,000 km) without major problems.

5 Diesel engines give better fuel economy than petrol. It's estimated that if all the cars in Europe ran on diesel, Europe's annual fuel bill would be halved. Average consumption from a good diesel is 40 mpg (14 km/litre), compared with 36 mpg (13 km/litre) for a similar petrol car.

6 Pick a good turbo-diesel car for better performance than most similarly-sized petrol engines, with 40 mpg (14 km/litre) fuel economy. The best TD cars are manufactured by Peugeot, Rover, Audi and Renault.

7 In the UK, diesel prices are set to come down as all of Europe moves fuel prices into line. Buy a diesel car now and within a year you could be paying around 20p per gallon (4p per litre) less than those people who run petrol-engined cars.

8 On the down side, two problems with diesels are its terrible smell and the way it sticks on the ground around the pump. To avoid slipping on the pedals, and to cut down the smell, keep an old pair of shoes in a plastic bag in the car. Slip them on when you fill up at a garage and then put them back in the bag when you drive away.

9 If you have a diesel car, try and use a filling station where they supply thin polythene gloves for drivers who use diesel. This simple measure means you don't go around all day with hands smelling of diesel.

10 It's a good idea for diesel car drivers to carry some form of scented wet-wipes to remove any lingering smell from their hands.

11 Diesel can froth when you're filling your car, and suddenly blow out of the tank when it's almost full. To avoid this, fill the last quarter of the tank really slowly, and stand to the side of the filler so that if it does froth at least you won't get it on your clothes.

12 If you have a petrol-engined car, when you're filling up make sure that you breathe as little of the fumes as you can because petrol contains benzene, small quantities of which are known to cause cancer if breathed for substantial periods. Scandinavian countries warn all drivers about this with a skull-and-crossbones motif on pumps.

Choosing an Economical Car

An economical car is not simply one which covers the greatest distance on the least fuel. Check the following if you want to ensure that the car you choose is amongst the most economical.

13 Don't pay too much attention to official government fuel figures because they are all somewhat misleading. Almost all these figures are achieved by running the car on a rolling road, with the car in top gear and travelling at a steady speed. The best guide is the urban or town driving figure, which is usually nearest to the fuel consumption you will achieve in normal driving conditions.

14 Check the quoted labour times for services – you will find these in the car's maintenance and service book, or the dealer should be able to tell you. These will give you a good idea of the cost of each service – but remember that parts and regular service items will be added on top, as will any purchase taxes.

15 Most major car manufacturers now have what's called menu pricing, which tells customers exactly how much set jobs cost. Check these out, because they give a good indication of general running costs.

16 Save money in the long run by buying a car which has long service intervals. Some makes still demand a trip to a dealer every 6,000 miles (10,000 km) – about every six months for most drivers – though an increasing number only demand that you come back every 12,000 miles (20,000 km), and some even stretch this to 20,000 miles (32,000 km), which could be every eighteen months for some drivers.

17 If you live in a major city, see if it will be possible to take your car a small distance away to a dealer in the country for its servicing. Hourly labour rates in a city can be double those in country areas.

18 Cut your annual motoring costs by choosing a model of car with a low insurance rating. First, the annual premium will be lower; and, just as important, most modern insurance rating systems worldwide take into account not only a car's performance but also its safety, security, likely repair costs, and cost of spare parts. So the lower the rating the less expensive the car will be to run, the safer it will be, and the harder it will be to steal!

Choosing a Safe Car

19 Be extra safe by choosing a light- or bright-coloured car. Dark-coloured cars are involved in around 20 per cent more accidents annually than vehicles in colours such as white, red, silver and bronze. The worst colour is dark blue, closely followed by dark green: these figure in the majority of accidents involving dark-coloured cars. Experts say it's because blue blends into most normal surroundings on the road far better than any other colour. The exception is a white car which, of course, can be virtually invisible in snow – so avoid white if you live in a place which has hard winters.

20 Look for these major safety features on any car you are considering buying. Many cars will have some of them, a few offer all: side impact steel door beams, roll cage, seat belt tensioners (they hold you more securely in the event of an accident), ABS anti-lock brakes, four wheel drive (gives twice as much grip when cornering), air bags (inflate out of the steering wheel during a major accident, cushioning the driver's head and stopping it hitting the steering wheel), Procon-Ten (an Audi patented device which automatically pulls the steering wheel out of the way if the car is involved in a really serious accident), traction control (helps keep grip when accelerating on slippery surfaces), ice-warning gauge and chime.

Choosing a Secure Car

21 A professional thief can break into most cars, but most cars are actually broken into by opportunist amateurs. Pick a car with one or more of these standard security features and your car will be harder to steal: key-operated engine immobilizer, deadlock door locks, shielded door locks, laser-cut keys (virtually impossible to copy), gear lever locked in reverse when the ignition key is removed (standard feature on Saabs), alarm system (preferably an ultrasonic system which protects windows as well as doors), a microwave alarm system on any convertible car (microwave alarm systems work best in convertibles – here, ultrasonics are a poor substitute and often give false alarms).

See also Chapters 6 and 7.

How to Pay for Your Car

There are a bewildering array of purchase schemes for both new and used cars. Choosing the one which best suits your particular circumstances takes care, but the right decision may save you lots of money.

22 When buying a new car check out the finance deal being offered by the dealer. The best schemes are those which offer low interest rates – beware of some '0 per cent' finance deals from the manufacturer. Check how much deposit you have to put down – often it's as much as 50 per cent – and check how long the 0 per cent is on offer for. Normally it's only for a year, so monthly payments are high.

23 It's best to pay a small deposit – usually the minimum is 10 per cent – and then get a low finance deal spread over three or four years. This way you get to keep most of your money and you can let it earn interest for you.

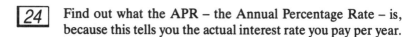

24 Find out what the APR – the Annual Percentage Rate – is, because this tells you the actual interest rate you pay per year.

25 Make sure the salesman can show you written proof of the APR – he is required to by law – because the much lower figure he will usually quote will often be the interest rate per month.

26 If buying secondhand, always try to pay cash because there are rarely low-interest deals in this market, and you can end up paying much more than the original price of the car in long-term interest payments.

27 If you cannot pay cash to buy a secondhand car, try and get a bank loan. This may charge the lowest interest rate you can get, and it will also be the safest form of loan.

Buying a New Car

Where to Buy

You can normally buy from a franchised car dealer, or you can go to a car broker. Which is best for you?

28 The franchised car dealer is an agent for the car manufacturer, so it is relatively easy to get some action if you are dissatisfied with your new car.

29 Franchised car dealers will generally have cars in stock, so you can look at them and drive them before you buy. You will also be able to negotiate a price, and arrange a loan if you need one, face-to-face.

30 Big savings can be had if you buy from a car broker because they work out of offices, rather than more costly showrooms, so they are able to offer lower prices – often as much as 12 – 15 per cent below those offered by a main franchised dealer.

31 Remember, though, that when it comes to servicing you have to take your car to the local dealer, and he may well be unhappy that you have gone to a broker rather than to him.

32 Get a price from a car broker and then ring round dealers – tell them the price you've been offered and see if they can match it. After a few calls you should find at least one dealer who will be prepared to match the broker's price.

Basic Tips

33 Whether buying new or secondhand, make sure you know as much as possible about the make and model of car you are going to see. Read what at least a couple of motoring magazines have to say about it. The salesman or vendor will then treat you with more respect, thus putting you in a stronger position when the time comes to talk money.

34 Even if you've set your heart on a brand-new car, don't close your eyes to ex-demonstration vehicles. These may only be a few months old and have covered a couple of hundred miles, yet they will be substantially less expensive – you could save as much as 15 – 20 per cent of the new price.

35 When you're considering a particular model of new car it's useful to check if it's about to be replaced. You can find this out by phoning the customer relations department of the manufacturer, who will be glad to tell you of any upcoming changes to their range. If you find your intended purchase is about to be phased out, you can negotiate a hefty discount. (Remember, however, that the 'outdated' car will lose value fairly quickly, so try and keep it for several years.)

When to Buy

36 In Britain, buy in September because some dealers may not have sold enough cars in August – when the registration year changes – so they may be keen to make a sale and will therefore offer you a bigger discount.

37 Alternatively, buy in June or July if you live in Britain – although you will be getting a car which does not carry the next year's registration letter, it will be cheaper as dealers will be keen to move it before the August rush on new registrations. (But remember, it will have a lower resale value than a car bought only a few weeks later with the new registration letter.)

38 If you live in a country or area with a distinct winter and summer season, and you want a convertible, buy during the winter months because dealers will offer higher discounts then. Conversely, don't buy a convertible in the summer when high demand will be matched by high prices and limited choice.

Dealers and Discounts

39 Before setting out to visit dealers, phone at least two for each make of car you are interested in. This may be more difficult in rural areas, but it's worth trying because one dealer may have a special offer going that his nearest competitor doesn't.

40 Save money by starting your phone calls or visits to dealers near the end of a month, because most dealers have monthly sales targets with cash incentives. If they have had a slack sales month so far, they may be prepared to drop their price to achieve their target.

41 Get hold of the car manufacturers' price lists for the cars you are interested in so that you know exactly how much they cost before you start to negotiate.

42 Always ask for a discount. In today's competitive world market hardly any car is sold for its full list price, so don't be embarrassed about asking. As a general rule, dealers get between 9 and 15 per cent commission per car, so they have room for manoeuvre if they are really keen to make a sale.

43 Remember, for every dealer who is unhelpful or unpleasant when you mention discounts there are many others who will be only too glad to have your business. Shop around.

44 On some cars which are selling well – makes such as BMW and Mercedes-Benz, some Rovers and Land Rover Discovery – there may be no major discount available. If there isn't, try for a low-rate finance package (*see 22 and 23*) or an added value package such as an extended warranty. If a dealer believes you are serious about buying he would rather offer extras such as these than see you taking your custom to another dealer down the road.

45 Don't try to do a deal over the phone, but ask a few pertinent questions. Have you got this car in stock? What colour choice do you have? If I buy from you could I have a courtesy car when mine's in for service? Are you offering any form of finance deal at the moment?

46 Visit the dealers who have been most helpful on the phone – these are usually the ones who will be prepared to spend as much time as you need, and they will usually come up with the most competitive deal. More often than not, a friendly salesman is a good pointer to a friendly service department – useful if problems occur once you've bought the car.

47 You can only get the biggest discounts if you go and visit the dealer in the showroom. But beware – this is the time when all the salesman's powers of persuasion will come into play. So be prepared to be pleasant but firm, and remember: there is almost always still room to haggle over the price.

48 Make sure you discuss a discount on the manufacturer's recommended price before you start talking about deposits, or how much your part-exchange car is worth. Once you've got some idea of the likely discount, then start talking about cheap-rate finance, how much the salesman will give you for your part-exchange car, and if he is prepared to throw in any extras such as an extended warranty package.

Test Drive and Other Checks

49 Car buyers often forget to have a really good look in the back, so check there's enough leg and headroom for your own and your passengers' needs. Check also that the boot is big enough.

50 If you are keen on a particular car make sure you go for a short test drive – amazingly, many people don't, and often they regret it later because the car they've chosen fails to live up to their expectations. Ask yourself if the car is quiet enough. Are all the controls in easy reach for you? Is the all-round visibility good? And, most importantly, is it comfortable and does the seat fit you well?

51 Remember that if something about the car annoys you on a short test drive, it will drive you completely mad when you have to live with the car day in, day out.

To Trade In or Not to Trade In?

52 It is better, on balance, to offer cash rather than a trade-in car because the dealer has to go to the trouble of selling the trade-in car before he realizes all his profit. So if you sell your old car privately – though it may take more time – you will get around 10 per cent more for it than if you sold it to a dealer. *See also Chapter 11*.

53 However, if you cannot afford the 10 per cent deposit that is usually demanded for a new car, this is the time when it makes most sense to offer your old car as a trade-in because it might cover the deposit and so save you having to borrow the cash.

54 If you are trading in your current car for a new one, you will get the best deal if you buy another of the same make. This is because the dealer knows exactly how much your old car is worth and he will find it easy to sell on his forecourt.

55 Before offering your car to a dealer in part exchange, make sure that you have a ball-park knowledge of its value, allowing for its current mileage and condition. Used-car price guides are published regularly and can be found at most newsagents.

56 Be prepared to juggle with the trade-in price if the dealer will offer you a fair discount on the new car. This makes you look reasonable and gives him the chance to appear charitable!

Closing the Deal

57 To stop car dealers adding on extras and hefty delivery charges after you've negotiated a price for the car, start off by finding out what the on-the-road price is and exactly what it includes.

58 Clinch a deal by making a realistic offer – you can get a good idea of discounts on your chosen car by looking at what's being offered at other dealerships. If you make too unrealistic an offer the salesman may well lose interest in you, considering you to be a time-waster. Make it clear that you are seriously interested in the car, but that you simply cannot afford to go to the full price he is asking. Then he will usually be prepared to negotiate, because he believes he will make a sale at the end of the day.

59 Don't be put off by a salesman who tells you that he has already had people in offering a higher price. If that were the case he would already have sold the car.

60 When negotiating, be polite and calm at all times. Try to build a rapport with the salesman, rather than fighting him.

61 If you put a deposit down on a new car, try and keep it as low as possible. Make sure that at the same time you sign a form of agreement which says you will get the deposit back if the car is not delivered by an agreed date.

Sorting Out the Details

62 It's often best to pick a car from the ones which the dealer has in his showroom, because he has already bought these vehicles from the manufacturer. If they have been there for some months he may have bought at a lower price, and may therefore be persuaded to lower his price to you.

63 Once you've agreed all the terms, go and pick up the car at the showroom because you can look round it and see if it's in tip-top condition. If not, reject it, or get the dealer to rectify any problems before you drive the car away.

64 If the dealer cannot or will not sort out any such problems, get in touch with the manufacturer – they all have customer relations staff who are there to help in such cases.

Car Brokers

65 Although there are big savings to be made on the price of a new car by buying from brokers, remember that they will rarely take your old car as a trade-in – so sell it privately.

66 If you buy through a broker, don't give him any money until you have the car – most brokers work out of offices and, unlike car dealers, the unscrupulous ones can disappear quickly.

67 Brokers buy cars through dealers. So, once the car is ready for delivery, try and pick it up rather than letting the broker do the job. This way you get to meet the dealer – whom you may well want to go back to in the future for servicing and maintenance. You can also check the car over to make sure it's in tip-top condition.

68 If a broker keeps putting the delivery date back and blames delays at the factory for the hold-up, get on the phone to the factory and find out if what he says is true.

Warranties and Guarantees

69 Make sure that you carefully examine the small print on any warranty or guarantee that you are offered, on both a new and a secondhand car.

70 When you are buying a car which has a warranty or guarantee with it – whether on a new or secondhand car – ask the seller or salesman to explain exactly what the warranty covers, and what its limitations are.

71 Take notes as the warranty is being explained to you – this will make the seller more careful about what he is telling you.

72 If you're buying a new car, try and get one with up to three years' mechanical warranty cover. Not only does this offer you extended protection should something go wrong, but it will also be a useful selling point if you want to sell before the three years is up.

73 You can keep your warranty in force by making sure that your car is serviced according to the service schedule. If it isn't, the warranty can be declared null and void if something does go wrong with the car.

74 Don't try to save money by getting your new car serviced by a smaller, independent dealer rather than by a franchised dealer. Doing so will nullify your warranty cover.

75 Anti-corrosion warranties do not guarantee against surface rust but only against rust coming through from underneath the bodywork, and the guarantee will become void if your local franchised dealer does not carry out regular checks. Make sure he does this at each service.

76 It's worth buying a new car which comes with a paintwork guarantee – usually they run for about six years – because any blemishes which might appear will be treated. This is also a sales plus for you when the time comes to sell the car.

Buying a Secondhand Car

Where to Buy

Buy from a main dealer for a wide choice of cars, often previously privately owned. You also have access to warranties (see page 33) and can easily test drive any car you are interested in. A dealer will also usually be prepared to take your present car in part exchange.

Buy from a private seller and the price will be lower than from a main dealer – often as much as 10 per cent less. But do check all documentation to make sure the car actually belongs to the seller – some unscrupulous traders masquerade as private sellers. Make sure also that the mileage is genuine, and that all servicing has been carried out up to date.

Buying at auction is not as dangerous as many people fear, and prices are generally lower here because this is where the car dealers buy. Follow the simple rules in 138–45 and you shouldn't go wrong.

General Tips

77 If you are buying a really old secondhand car – say around ten years old or more – make sure it is a common make in your country. If you buy a car this old it's important to be able to find spare parts easily.

78 If buying privately, take an appropriate insurance cover note with you so that you can have a short test drive.

79 If buying from a dealer, look for membership of a trade association. Then, if you have problems soon after buying, you can get the trade body to help you sort them out.

80 Even if you are convinced that the car you are looking at is absolutely the one for you, tell the vendor that you'll sleep on it. Invariably he will call you the next day, and most often will soon get round to discussing a drop in price.

Inspection

81 Never go and see any car which you are thinking of buying if it's raining or getting dark. It may seem obvious, but many buyers do just this and all too often end up with a car whose faults may well have been hidden in the darkness, only to be starkly revealed the day after they've bought it.

82 Never be hurried when looking over a secondhand car. Remember, there are other vehicles out there if the one you are looking at is not exactly what you want. If there is even a glimmer of doubt in your mind, walk away and look elsewhere. It may take a little longer, but if you have patience the right car will always come along.

83 When you go to inspect a secondhand car, wear old clothes and take a small mat and a torch. Then you can crawl under the car and have a good look for any underbody corrosion.

84 Carry a small magnet and run it over the main bodywork panels. If there is any area to which it isn't attracted, the bodywork may well have been damaged and badly repaired with filler. However, some modern cars have major plastic body parts – for example, the bonnet of the Citroen BX is plastic – so do some research before you get the magnet out!

85 Paying for a professional (such as a representative of a motoring organisation) to check the car over is nothing compared with the cost of most cars – it's money well spent. If the seller refuses to let you arrange such a check, then don't walk away – run. There's definitely a problem with this car, and it's likely to be quite a serious one.

Documents and Other Proofs of Authenticity

86 If you are buying privately the vendor should have all the relevant documents to hand, and he must let you see them. Double check that the colour of the car, its registration number, its mileage and the name of the seller all tie up with the documents.

87 Surprising though it may seem, I have talked to several people who have bought cars whose service books have had pages ripped out! At the very least this points to a clocked car whose mileage is not genuine *(see 120–2)*, and it could even indicate a written-off car which has been rebuilt. Never buy a car – no matter how attractive the price – if it comes with a service book which is anything less than genuine-looking and complete.

88 When buying privately, never buy from someone if their name is not on the registration document. This can mean that the car has been stolen, or that the vendor is a dealer posing as a private person. Whatever the reason, there could be more to this car than meets the eye.

89 If a vendor tells you that he cannot show you the relevant documents when you are looking at the car, but that he will have them for you when you pick the car up, get your running shoes on – this car is not all that it seems.

90 A useful piece of paper to have, especially from a private seller, is the original purchase document – though if all the other relevant documents are there this is one you can live without.

91 If the car is marked with window security etching – showing either the registration or the chassis number – check that this tallies. If it does not, you may well be looking at a stolen car.

92 It's worth finding out if the secondhand car you are looking at has any finance outstanding on it. If it has, technically the car does not belong to you, even if you've bought it quite legally. There are companies who can tell you, for a fee, if there is still finance owed or if the car has been stolen. At the time of writing these services were only just becoming available to the general public.

93 If buying privately, make sure that you actually go inside the seller's house to look at documents. It is not unusual for unscrupulous trade sellers to park the car outside someone else's house; then as you turn up they walk down the pathway towards you. You believe they live there, but when you've bought the car the seller disappears. Not surprisingly, there are often serious problems with any car sold this way.

94 It's not a good idea to let the seller bring the car to your own home – it could be a stolen car, and he could easily give a false name and address.

95 If you're buying a secondhand car from a dealer, once you have seen the documentation of the vehicle you are interested in, ring the previous owner to see if the mileage is genuine.

Closing the Deal – Final Checks

96 If buying privately, take someone else along with you as a witness, and write down anything which the seller tells you about the car. Then you will have a record, and he will realize it's not worth telling you overt lies about the car.

97 If a sound system is fitted, make sure it's included in the price – it's not safe just to assume it will be.

98 When you buy the car, make sure that the seller – whether it's a dealer or a private person – gives you a receipt (with their full name and address on) which states exactly what you are buying, the precise mileage, the registration and what you have paid. If there is a dispute later, at least you can prove that you bought the car in good faith – a good basic legal point.

How to Spot a Good (and Bad) Secondhand Car

○ *Bodywork, Engine and Other Mechanical Parts*

99 Ask yourself if the colour and texture of the paintwork match all over. If they don't, there has been a full or partial respray. This can mean accident damage, or corrosion underneath the paintwork. Look for paint over-spray on the window rubbers or around the headlights – a sure sign that the car has been resprayed. Ask yourself why the car has been resprayed.

100 Check that the gaps between the body panels are even. If they are not, this could indicate badly repaired accident damage. Or, more seriously, it could even be a vehicle which has been built from several other crashed cars.

101 Look along the sides for any rippled body panels, another sign that the car has been badly damaged.

102 Look under the bonnet or hood for any rippling of the metal along the insides of the engine bay, or bad welds, or a poor fit to the panels. All of these signal accident damage, and therefore a car that is best avoided.

103 A good basic engine check is to lift the oil filler cap and see if there is any creamy-white gunge on it. If so, it is likely that the cylinder head gasket is leaking. This can sometimes be cured by replacing the gasket, but if it has been left too long serious damage could have occurred to the engine.

104 Listen carefully for an engine that sounds very rattly when ticking over. This is usually a sign that the camshaft bearings are worn, which could herald expensive repairs. Best to look for another car.

105 When looking under the car – with the aid of a torch – look for rust or damage to the underside. A good check here is to see if the jacking points – used to jack the car up – are corroded. If they are, there could well be further serious corrosion problems, because these are normally the strongest parts of the car.

106 While you are under the car, check the brake fluid pipes for any leaks, and also – if the car is front wheel drive – look for any rips in the rubber boots over the front axles (near the wheels). If it's a rear wheel drive car, look for oil leaks from the drive shaft on the rear axle. Any leaks in these areas will require expensive repairs.

107 An easy check to make for worn suspension joints, or worn wheel bearings, is to get hold of each wheel at top and bottom and tug it. Any slackness there points to problems with parts of the suspension, or with the steering.

108 Check for play in the steering – with the engine turned on so that power steering, if the car has it, can operate. If there is more than an inch of play (about 3cm) before the driving wheels start to turn there may well be something wrong with the track rod ends – a potentially expensive problem.

109 Listen for a clunking noise when moving the steering from side to side. There could be problems with the steering joints – another potentially expensive repair.

110 Power steering systems – especially those over five years old – tend to hiss when the steering wheel is turned full over. But if you hear a groaning noise at such times there could well be a problem with the motor, or a leak somewhere in the system.

111 Check the condition of the driver's seat to get a good idea of how much wear and tear the car has suffered. This is better than just looking at the condition of the pedal rubbers. If they are worn, so the argument goes, the car has probably covered high mileage – but pedal rubbers can easily be replaced. It's less likely that an owner will have replaced the seat.

112 Is there an assortment of different tyres? If so, this suggests an owner who has not really cared for his car.

113 Take a close look at alloy wheels. If they are scuffed – usually as a result of careless parking – this tells you that the previous driver was quite careless with his car. Scuffed wheels also alert you to the possibility that the steering geometry could be damaged. Finally, regular kerbing of alloy wheels can cause tiny fractures in the alloy, eventually leading to the potentially disastrous scenario of the wheel breaking up as you drive!

114 Are there too many keys? If there are, it means the car has had new door locks fitted. This in turn means that it's probably been broken into, or even been involved in a serious accident.

115 Look for any bodywork corrosion in the most common places: bottoms of the doors, along the tops of the front wings, creeping from under the side trim, along sills, around wheel arches, along body seams, under the carpet at the front, and around the suspension mounts under the bonnet (hood).

116 Look very closely at a car which has bubbles on its paintwork. These indicate rust creeping through, a far more serious problem than mere scratches. Rust bubbles point to poor metal, poor paintwork – and problems ahead.

117 Look out for freshly applied underseal under the car or on the sills, because this can very often hide rusty areas. And if you see it inside the engine bay there is almost certainly a big problem – the car could be an insurance write-off which has been put back together badly.

118 Check in the radiator to see if the water is either clear (no anti-freeze) or green or blue (contains anti-freeze). If it's brown, corrosion has taken hold and could lead to further problems. Severe corrosion may already have resulted in engine damage.

119 Look inside the boot or trunk for any knocks or scrapes, or damaged paintwork. This suggests a careless owner, or that the car has had a hard life carrying heavy objects.

120 If you are looking at a car with a five-figure mileometer, check very carefully that it has not done over 100,000 miles, or kilometres, by carefully examining all the documents and looking at the general condition of the car. Why? Because once over 100,000 the mileometer goes back to 0. A high-mileage vehicle used as a business car could well have covered 130,000 within four or five years; but you may look at the mileometer and simply consider that this is a good car because it's only covered, say, 30,000 miles. Most modern cars have six-figure mileometers.

121 Check carefully for figures that don't quite line up on the mileometer. This is often a sign that it has been tampered with and the figures wound back.

122 Check the screws, and their surrounds on the mileometer, to see if they appear to have been tampered with – another sign of clocking.

123 Make sure all the warning lights are working – they should all come on when the ignition key is turned one notch. It's unfortunately all too easy for an unscrupulous seller to disconnect a wire.

Test Drive

124 Take at least a 10 mile (16 km) test drive, because it could take that long for faults such as worn gearbox synchromesh to show up. The seller shouldn't mind you taking a test drive of this length if the car is OK. If he is not happy, ask yourself why . . .

125 On a manual car, check for a worn clutch during the test drive. Dip the clutch when you're driving along in fourth or fifth gear and rev the engine. Keep it revving and then let the clutch out. The revs should drop instantly, and the car pull cleanly. If it is still revving, the clutch is past its best and will soon need replacing.

126 Listen carefully when trying to change gear. If you hear any crunching noises, especially on second and third which are the gears most often used, be cautious. Such noises mean that the gear syncromesh is badly worn – a problem which will only get worse.

127 Clonking noises when you slow down or accelerate are not good news. It could just be loose engine mounts – not expensive to replace – but it could also be the far more serious problem of worn drive shafts.

128 Listen out for a clicking noise when accelerating with the steering wheel turned full left or right. This means that the constant velocity joints are worn – these are the joints which pass the power from the engine to the wheels. An expensive repair.

129 If the brakes seem to have a lot of travel in the pedal, and also feel rather spongy, and if when you pump them the bite point happens sooner then you expect, then there's probably a leak somewhere in the braking system and it could be expensive to repair.

130 When you're driving, listen out for any rattles or squeaks. These are often really hard to track down, let alone get rid of. Don't underestimate this problem, because over time it will drive you mad.

131 Suspension should soak up bumps without continuing to bounce the car after you have driven back on to smoother ground. If the bounce continues, the suspension dampers need replacing.

132 Any noisy crashing from the suspension points to worn suspension bushes. This problem is not expensive to repair, and should be expected on a high-mileage car. But check this out if it's encountered on a car with apparently low mileage, because it points to a vehicle which has actually done far more.

133 When you return from the test drive, look under the bonnet again for any signs of oil or water leaks, and get the seller to blip the accelerator while you look for excessive smoke from the exhaust and listen for any engine misfires.

○ *Documents and Similar Checks*

134 Check the car's equipment carefully against the original manufacturer's specification because there have been cases of sellers changing a car's badges – uprating a car from an L to a GL, for example. Look on the registration documents to find out exactly which version the vehicle is supposed to be.

135 If the car is said to have a reconditioned engine, ask to see the bill and warranty cover – it's easy to steam-clean an old engine and then paint it to make it look like a reconditioned one.

136 Service histories can be forged by getting a blank book, making up a cheap rubber stamp and then falsifying the service stamps. Check with previous owners that the information in the book is correct.

137 When you are checking through the service documents look for any mention of camshaft belt replacement, especially if the car you are looking at has covered more than 35,000 miles (56,500 km). This is important because worldwide around 13 per cent of breakdowns are caused by cam belt failure, usually because they have not been replaced early enough. A failed belt can seriously damage the engine, so check whether it has been replaced or is due for replacement.

Buying at Auction

138 Visit a couple of auctions without going along to buy. This way you will get a good idea of how the system works, you can see how much the type of car you are interested in is selling for, and you'll become accustomed to the fast selling pace. Don't take your cheque book, credit card or any cash. That way you can observe without getting sucked into the buying action – at least until you know what you are doing.

139 Narrow your choice of car down to a maximum of three, and then stick to them. Don't make the mistake of suddenly falling in love with a car which looks attractively priced but which isn't really what you want.

140 Cars will normally be started up about fifteen minutes before they enter the auction ring. Make sure you stand near the car you are interested in so that you can see if it starts easily, or if the engine sounds rattly, or if there are clouds of black smoke coming out of the exhaust. This is the only chance you will get.

141 Ask for information from the big auction companies about the spread of prices you should expect to pay for specific models of car. These values are compiled weekly by computer, based on prices fetched at previous auctions for specific cars. Armed with this information, you will have a better idea of relative values when you come to start bidding.

142 When you feel confident enough to bid, make sure you get along there an hour or two before bidding starts. This should give you time to zero-in on the cars you are interested in. You won't be able to drive them, but you can run their engines and listen for any untoward noises. You should also check the bodywork carefully for any accident damage.

143 Set yourself a spending limit, and then stick to it. Don't go just over your self-imposed limit, because if you do you may suddenly find yourself bidding higher and higher until you are in way above your head.

144 Don't worry too much about high mileage (80,000 miles/130,000 km-plus) as long as the car has a full service history and looks to have good bodywork and sturdy interior trim. Most of today's cars will happily cover over 100,000 miles (160,000 km) before any serious problems occur.

145 Look for cars with any form of warranty still in force. These will be slightly more expensive, but at least you will have some protection should anything go wrong. This is important because auction companies hardly ever offer guarantees of their own.

Warranties and Guarantees

146 Be very careful about purchasing a warranty when you buy a secondhand car – the small print often says that you have to pay for any repairs first and then reclaim the cost from the insurance company backing the warranty.

147 Some of the best warranties on secondhand cars are provided by the car manufacturers themselves on selected used cars – usually those up to two years old. Search for these because they are very similar to the extensive cover you get on a new vehicle, and they will enhance the resale value of the car.

For general points on warranties see 69–76.

Checks, Maintenance and Servicing

Checking Your New Car

Now that you've got your car, make sure it's always in good condition by performing these regular checks.

○ *Lights*

148 If you have no one to help you, check your rear lights are working by backing up close to a wall at night. When you brake, look in your mirrors to see if both red lamps are lighting up the wall. Similarly, you can use this method to see if your rear fog lights, and each direction indicator, are working.

○ *Oil*

149 Check your car's oil level every week, or when you take a break midway through a long, high-speed journey. At high speeds oil can burn rapidly, and if your car is regularly used in congested city streets the oil thins so much that engine protection may be lost if the level is allowed to drop too low.

150 Let the car stand for several minutes before you check the oil level, because during this time oil will still be slowly seeping back down from the top of the engine to the bottom – into the engine's sump – so you will not get a true reading unless you wait.

151 When checking the oil, do it twice, wiping the dipstick with a clean cloth between each check. This way you can be sure that the reading is correct – some types of dipstick collect oil in the pipe, and the first time the dipstick is drawn out it can bring some of this oil with it, so giving a false reading.

○ *Water and Anti-freeze*

152 Check your car's water level every week. However, owners of cars such as the Volkswagen Beetle and Citroen 2CV should not waste their time searching for the water radiator, because their cars are air-cooled!

153 When checking the water level, never take the cap off the radiator just after the car has been driven because scalding hot water will gush out. Remember that the water is under considerable pressure and so it takes a long time to cool down – as much as an hour.

154 If you have to take the radiator cap off when the engine is still warm – though this can never be recommended, and it's hard to see a necessary circumstance – wrap a thick cloth all around the top of the cap and the edges of the radiator. Then slowly unscrew the top, keeping plenty of pressure bearing down on it so that the sudden pressure increase does not blow it off like a bullet. Any escaping hot water should be absorbed by the cloth.

155 On most modern cars, the water level can easily be checked without taking the radiator cap off. Follow the small hose from the top of the radiator to the small transparent plastic expansion bottle, then check the level against the minimum and maximum markings.

156 Rock the car gently when checking the water level in the expansion bottle, just in case there's an air-lock somewhere in the system. This is especially important if the car has been standing for some time in hot weather.

157 If the car has overheated for some reason and most of the water has steamed out, remember that, if you live in a northern climate, when you replace the water you should add the right amount of anti-freeze. In an increasing number of modern cars anti-freeze is added when the car is manufactured and is then sealed in with the water, only being checked for strength annually by the dealer. Such mixtures have been specially designed to stop corrosion of the cooling system, so it's imperative that they are replaced with the recommended anti-freeze.

○ *Batteries*

158 Car batteries last for two to three years, not the lifetime that many drivers assume, so check yours each week by lifting each of the cell covers – or the single plastic strip which covers each row of cells – to make sure that the water level is right up. If you keep the water at this level the battery will last longer than if it's neglected.

159 Only distilled water – available from all garages – should be used in a battery. Never use ordinary tap water, which will almost immediately destroy the battery's ability to work properly.

○ Tyres

It's very important to check your tyres because ultimately those small patches of rubber are all that keeps you on the road, so they must be in first-class condition.

160 Different countries have differing legal minima for tyre tread depth. Make sure you know what they are in your country, and in any other countries you are visiting in your car.

161 If you hear a regular clicking noise as you drive it may be just a stone stuck in the tread of one of your tyres (which can easily be removed with a fingernail or screwdriver), but it could also be a nail or screw. Check this out immediately, because if so it will soon work itself loose and at high speed could suddenly explode the tyre, causing you to lose control of your car.

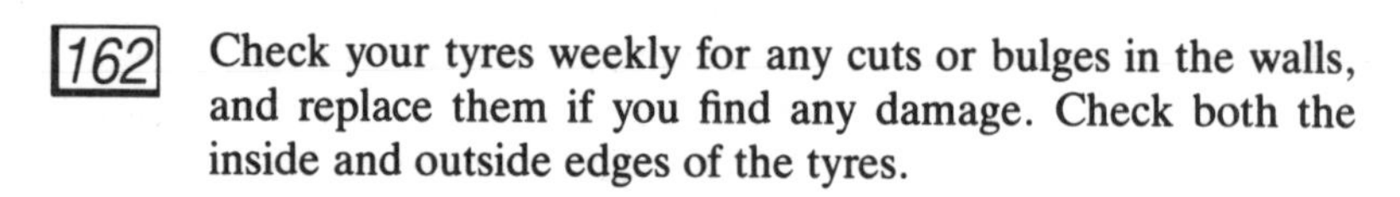

162 Check your tyres weekly for any cuts or bulges in the walls, and replace them if you find any damage. Check both the inside and outside edges of the tyres.

163 Bulges in tyre sidewalls are most often caused by careless kerbing – knocking the wheels against the kerb when parking – and this can lead to the tyre exploding at high speeds. What happens is that the steel wires inside radial tyres become deformed, so destroying the tyre's rigidity and strength.

164 If you notice any uneven tread wear on the front tyres it's usually due to poor tracking or balancing of the wheels, and is easily cured by a tyre agent or dealer. It must be carried out as soon as possible, though – while it is rarely dangerous, it will wear the tyres very quickly.

165 Wear right in the middle of the tread, and around most of the tyre, means that the tyre pressures are too high. Refer to your car's handbook and reset the pressures.

166 Wear around both edges of the tyre usually means that the tyre pressures are too low. Reset them at the right pressure.

167 Check tyre pressures each week, and make sure that they are correct (look in the handbook).

168 It's a good idea to use the same filling station's tyre pressure pump each time, because different pumps' readings can vary slightly.

169 Make sure you either use a pump near to your home, or else let the tyres cool before testing for pressure. Driving for any distance heats the tyres up and will give you a false reading.

170 Don't over-inflate your car's tyres to give a tauter ride – it can cause the tyres to explode at high speed or when cornering.

171 Don't under-inflate your tyres either, because this causes excessive flexing of the tyre's structure and rapid overheating, leading to break-up of the tyre's casing – usually at high speeds.

172 If you are driving with a full load, check the handbook to find out if the tyre pressures should be increased. Normally they should be, because with a full load the tyres are effectively running under-inflated. Don't forget to reduce the pressures again once the load has been taken out of your car.

Other Basic Checks

173 Find out the maximum permitted payload for your car, and do not exceed it. Remember that you will have to take the combined weight of passengers into account as well as any luggage.

174 Check your windscreen washer fluid level and make sure that in winter it contains enough anti-freeze so that it doesn't turn to ice as it hits the windscreen.

175 Before any long journey, quickly check the following: all lights are working, you have enough fuel, the oil and water levels are at the right level, your tyre pressures are correct, you have your wallet, money, cheque book and credit cards. Make sure that all your windows and your lights are clean.

○ *Checks to Make in Winter Months*

176 Check the level of anti-freeze in your car's water system. This can most easily be done by looking at the colour of the water. Most anti-freeze solutions colour the water either bright blue or green.

177 It's a good idea always to carry a can of de-icer in your car, but check the label carefully before you buy because some of the cheaper ones contain highly corrosive chemicals which may damage your paintwork.

178 If you don't like the thought of spraying corrosive de-icer on your car's windscreen – and if the thought of accidentally breathing in the fumes strikes you as even more objectionable – use the edge of a credit car to scrape the ice off. Most times it'll do nicely!

179 If your windscreen is frozen check that the wipers are not stuck in the ice before you switch them on, because if they cannot move they may burn their motor out – it is best to clean the screen first. The same applies, of course, if you have a rear screen wiper.

Servicing

180 If your car is still under guarantee or warranty don't over-run the service schedules, even by a few hundred miles or kilometres. Not only is there more chance of something going wrong, but failing to stick to service schedules can make the warranty null and void if something does go wrong.

181 If your car is under five years old make sure it's serviced by fully trained mechanics, and stick to the regular service intervals. It will cost more than doing the work yourself but in the long run you will save money because the car will be kept in tip-top condition. However once your car is five years old, and if it's only used for very low mileage, you can save money by doing the basic work yourself.

182 Keep your car for over 80,000 miles (130,000 km) and you will find it begins to cost less per mile to keep on the road than before. This is because items such as tyres, exhaust, brakes and even shock absorbers are all likely to have been changed before then.

See also 74.

Choosing Tools

If you are going to do the servicing yourself (and even for basic maintenance) you need a good basic set of tools.

183 Make sure you have a set of screwdrivers in assorted sizes and lengths and that there's a mix of flat blade and cross-head designs. Choose screwdrivers with rubber-coated handles because these are the safest if you accidentally touch a high-voltage electric lead in the engine bay.

184 A socket set with interchangeable heads is central to any decent toolkit. Spend a reasonable sum, because some of the cheaper versions are made of poor-quality metal which soon fractures. The best are usually nickel-coated.

185 A plug-spanner for unscrewing your car's spark plugs is very useful, but before you buy find out exactly which size you need – if the fit is too tight you could snap a plug when trying to remove it, and then it's near impossible to get the damaged plug out of the engine block.

186 A set of good spanners is essential – buy the ones with a ring at one end and an open end at the other. Though the size will be the same, the different end designs mean each spanner can be used in a variety of ways – useful in the sometimes cluttered engine bays of modern cars.

187 Buy at least two pairs of pliers – a sturdy blunt-ended pair, and a long-nose pair. The former is for strength, the long-nosed pair for reaching into awkward places.

188 A self-grip wrench is a useful addition to any toolkit, because once attached and locked on it leaves your hands free for other tasks.

189 Today an increasing number of cars have socket-headed bolts for some parts, so buy a set of hexagon keys for undoing them.

190 Feeler gauges are useful for adjusting the gaps on engine valves (on older cars) and spark plug gaps. These days most sets include both metric and imperial sizes.

191 If you intend to change your engine oil yourself you will also need a drain plug tool, preferably a multi-ended one so that you can unplug both your radiator – when you want to change the water – and your engine sump to let the oil flow out. If you cannot find one of these, you may find that a strong ring spanner will do the job.

Simple DIY Maintenance

Basic tasks which most averagely competent mechanics can consider include changing oil and water; checking and changing spark plugs; changing clutch fluid, oil and air filters, and burnt-out fuses.

192 Find out where your car's fuse box is. Even if you don't intend to do any work on the car yourself, it's important to know where the fuses are and where the spares are placed in the box.

193 If a fuse blows, get the car checked over by a professional mechanic as soon as possible – it could be a sign of other problems in the car's electrical system.

194 When looking into the engine compartment, always keep anything loose out of the way – tie back long hair, keep ties and scarves well clear, and take off any jewellery. Many cars today have electric engine fans and that means they can switch on automatically, even when the engine has been turned off. If your tie, for example, got caught in the fan you could be killed. Metal jewellery can also cause injury if it touches a high-voltage part of the engine such as the battery.

195 Keep your battery in tip-top condition by checking it over once a month. Ensure it is clean and secure. Remove any corrosion and clean the terminals, then smear them with protective petroleum jelly before tightening the leads. Check that the earth lead or strap is in good condition and secure.

196 You are less likely to suffer a breakdown if you regularly check the coolant and heater hoses, checking for softening caused by oil spills, splits in the hoses, and loose clips.

197 It's a good idea to check the tension of the fanbelt by pressing your thumb into the centre of it. If the belt gives no more than about 3/4 inch (1.5 cm) it is all right. Any more and it needs tightening.

198 If your car has a winter/summer setting on the air intake, make sure it is turned to the right seasonal setting.

Keeping Your Car Clean

199 When washing your car, don't be tempted to use ordinary household washing-up liquid because this will badly smear the windows when it rains, making sudden wet-weather driving extremely hazardous.

200 Don't use ordinary household spray cleaners on interior glass because when you are driving it can soon cause the windscreen to mist over, and when you wipe it the glass may smear. Use a proper glass cleaner, preferably one specially made for car use.

201 If your car is really dirty, hose it down before using a sponge on it – a sponge easily traps grit, which then scours the paintwork as you clean. Hosing first will remove most of the serious grit.

202 Wash your car with lukewarm water and start with the roof, working your way down. This allows the water to start loosening any grit or grime still left on the lower bodywork, which in turn means there's less chance of you scratching the paintwork when you come to sponge the lower reaches.

203 Make doubly sure that the door undersides and sills are cleaned properly, because this is where corrosion can start if the paint and bodywork are not well looked after.

204 It's better for the paintwork if you wash it by hand (and cheaper, and better for your health too!). If you use a drive-through car-wash often the brushes will soon leave swirling marks on your car's paintwork.

205 If you do use a car-wash, remember your car's aerial! Roof-mounted aerials can usually be unscrewed, but if not, lay the aerial flat against the roof and hope the brushes don't rip it off.

206 Save money on car polish by washing with a wax car cleaner and then rinsing with fresh, clean water. Finally, wipe over with a chamois leather – the finish will be mirror-like.

207 Use special car paintwork cleaning liquids sparingly, because these petrol-based solutions clean by taking off a thin layer of paint. If they are used regularly you will lose the shine, and the finish will become very patchy.

208 It's not a good idea to use any form of polish on a car less than two months old. The paintwork may not yet have hardened sufficiently, and so polish will simply strip off the outer protective layer. This is also the case with any areas of the car which have just been resprayed.

209 When cleaning your car, if you find any scratches going right through the paintwork clean them thoroughly – gently scraping any surface rust off with a knife – and then treat with a rust neutralizer. After that lightly apply a primer and finish with the car's own colour (obtainable from dealers or car accessory shops), building up several coats of paint to give good overall protection.

210 To get a good paint finish, let each coat dry completely, then rub it down gently with wet-and-dry abrasive paper before applying the next coat.

Annual Spring Clean

Once a year, give the underside of your car a good clean after first raising it as high as possible on supported ramps.

211 Wear a pair of goggles to protect your eyes when removing dirt from underneath the car.

212 To scrape off loose dirt, don't use a knife – use a wallpaper scraper or piece of wood. These are less likely to break through any underbody sealant.

213 When cleaning underneath the car, pay particular attention to wheel arches and any crevices where dirt has lodged and collected.

214 Once loose dirt has been removed, hose down the underside of the car. While it is drying look for any leaks and check body seam welds, rubber grommets and rubber wheel gaiters. Use a sealing compound on small leaks and replace old, leaking gaiters.

215 While you are under the car, examine all the exhaust mountings to make sure they are holding the exhaust properly in place. Check also for any corrosion in the exhaust system.

216 Carry out a careful check of all pipes, cables and linkages for any damage or corrosion.

217 If the car is undersealed, see if the coating is in good condition. If you notice any bare spots, clean the area with a wire brush and take out any rust. Apply new underseal. Remember, though, that if your car is covered by a bodywork corrosion warranty the terms might specify how such repairs should be carried out.

Special Checks

218 Although hardly a regular servicing item, it is important to change the camshaft belt every 35,000 miles (56,500 km). If you don't the belt can snap, which will cause serious damage to the engine. Replacement is not expensive – a mere fraction of the cost of engine repairs.

219 When checking the oil, if you see any globules of water on your dipstick it's wise to get a garage to check the car because this is a sign of water getting into the oil. This is usually the result of a worn engine head gasket, which can eventually cause more serious engine problems. Repair, if caught early enough, is quick and not expensive.

220 If the oil is low – this can easily happen after a long, high-speed journey – make sure your engine is topped up with the right type of oil. The handbook will list the recommended types. The wrong oil may be either too thick or too thin. Thicker-than-recommended oil can cause engine sludge to build up, which could affect the engine's performance, while too thin oil may not properly protect the engine, and so cause premature wear.

221 If you notice a smell like rotten eggs when driving, the battery may have overheated – this is rare, but it can happen when there's an electrical problem. Stop the car and investigate, because in extreme cases the battery can explode. (This advice is especially important if you have a British Austin Mini made in the 1980s – its battery is in the boot (trunk) of the car, near the fuel tank. If the battery is bubbling, don't breathe the fumes for they are extremely caustic and can damage your lungs. Wait for the battery to stop bubbling and then drive slowly to the nearest garage, stopping often if the smell returns. (NB Petrol-engined cars fitted with catalytic converters produce a smell like rotten eggs from their exhausts. This is normal, and no cause for concern.)

222 If the water in your radiator is a dirty brown it's probably because there is serious corrosion in the cooling system. This can cause two problems: first, poor water circulation, leading to engine overheating, and second, contaminated and therefore useless anti-freeze.

223 If your car's cooling system keeps overheating, and it has brown water in it, the system should be drained and refilled with clean water mixed with anti-freeze to protect against further corrosion.

224 If you are going to change the water make sure that the car's engine is cold – it should be left overnight.

225 To empty the radiator, reach under the car to the bottom of the radiator. You will find a small screw-in plug. Unscrew this and the dirty water will flow out. Flush the system through several times with clean water, until the water coming out is clean. Top up with clean water and the right level of anti-freeze (details will be in your car's handbook).

226 If you are putting your own engine anti-freeze in, check the label carefully because cheaper anti-freezes are often highly flammable. Although in winter they work well, if your engine gets too hot in the summer the anti-freeze can ignite and set fire to the engine.

227 If you are going on a long journey – perhaps driving in another country for some weeks on holiday – don't have your car serviced just before you go, but several weeks earlier. Why? It gives any new and replacement parts time to bed-in properly, and there will also be time for you to discover if the mechanics haven't done their job properly, or even left tools under the bonnet (hood). It happens!

Cutting the Cost of Driving

228 Keep your car in tip-top mechanical condition to ensure it is running economically and therefore saving you money.

229 Stick to the recommended service intervals, and have the car maintained by professional mechanics. This might cost a little more than doing it yourself, but ultimately you will see savings, thanks to better fuel economy and greater long-term reliability.

On the Road

230 If your car has a manual choke don't keep it pulled out any longer than you need, because a full-out choke can make your fuel consumption rise alarmingly. In addition, a full-out choke enriches the fuel mixture so much that it can strip the protective film of oil from the engine's pistons, so causing premature engine wear.

231 If your car has an automatic choke, save money by quickly blipping the throttle to the floor after you've covered around 2 miles (3 km). This will cut off the fuel-thirsty choke sooner than it will normally switch off automatically. Result: substantial fuel savings.

232 The secret of economy driving is to drive smoothly at all times. Sudden acceleration or braking has a serious effect on fuel consumption, so plan ahead so that you can better anticipate when you will need to slow down or stop.

233 Get into the highest gear possible as quickly as you can. The higher the gear the less work the engine has to do, so fuel consumption is much improved. But don't let the engine labour in too high a gear, because this will actually use more fuel than if you were in a lower gear. The moral is, use the correct gear at all times.

234 Consider an automatic geared car if most of your driving is around town. Left to its own devices, an auto picks the best, most economical gear at all times, and this also causes less wear and tear to the engine.

235 Always try and pick the least congested route from A to B – it is always more economical in terms of tyre wear, fuel economy, and general wear and tear on the car.

Tyres

236 Make sure your car's tyre pressures are correct. Under-inflation by 20 per cent cuts a tyre's life by 26 per cent, while 20 per cent over-inflation will cut a tyre's life by 10 per cent.

237 Low tyre pressures create more drag and therefore increase fuel consumption.

See also 172.

238 If you live in a very hot country, you will substantially increase the life of your car's tyres if you only go out when the temperature is at its lowest! Taking 60°F (16°C) as a typical ambient temperature, at 40°F (4°C) tyre life can double, but at 90°F (32°C) it can be halved.

239 Remember that tyres wear out almost twice as fast at 70 mph (112 kph) than they do at 35 mph (56 kph).

240 About every 12,000 miles (19,000 km) get a specialist tyre centre to rotate your wheels, swapping those at the front with those at the back. This will make all four tyres last that much longer, because most modern radials are good for 25,000 miles (40,000 km) on the driving wheels, and as much as 60,000 miles (96,000 km) on the other wheels. At the same time make sure the wheels are properly and professionally balanced again, otherwise the tyres will quickly wear and the steering will be affected.

241 When you have new tyres fitted, give them some time to bed-in properly. For the first 100 miles (160 km) don't exceed about 50 mph (80 kph), and the tyres will ultimately last longer.

242 Avoid 'nearly new' tyres, as they are often called – indeed, in some countries they are illegal. 'Nearly new' often means that they have come from written-off cars – though they may be cheap, they could well have internal damage which you may not know about until the tyre explodes at high speed. Remember that when you are driving, each tyre has only as much tread as the palm of your hand in contact with the road.

Fuel

243 Driving with the windows even slightly open, especially at motorway speeds, can increase fuel consumption by as much as 20 per cent. Similarly, try not to have your sunroof open if you don't really need it, because that too creates extra drag and therefore increases fuel consumption.

244 If possible, try and get all your luggage in the boot (trunk). A full roof-rack dramatically worsens the air-flow over the car's body, making it about as aerodynamic as a house brick and consequently very uneconomical.

245 Removing the roof-rack when it is not needed can save as much as 20 per cent on your annual fuel bill.

246 Work out routes which avoid heavy traffic. During stop-start town driving you can use 100 per cent more fuel than when driving in top gear on an uncongested road.

247 Don't fill up if a tanker is on the filling station forecourt topping up the main tank. Rainwater can often get mixed with petrol at these times, and if you fill up with adulterated fuel your tank may later have to be completely drained and the fuel wasted.

248 If you want a diesel-engined car, carefully read the information about servicing before you buy. Some diesel cars demand a service every 4,500 miles (7,000 km), compared with 12,000 miles (19,000 km) for most petrol-engined cars. Savings in fuel may be wiped out by servicing bills.

249 Don't shop around too far from home in the search for the cheapest fuel because you may cancel out any savings by having to drive further.

250 On hot days, or in hot climates, try and park in the shade because petrol evaporates when hot and you can lose a significant amount of fuel this way.

False Economies

251 Don't try to save money on insurance premiums by being economical with the truth. In other words, don't say your car is garaged overnight if it isn't, because if the car is stolen and it has not been garaged your insurance cover will be invalid. *See also Chapter 7.*

252 Don't make the mistake of trying to save money by buying cheap spare parts (which may be counterfeits) or engine oil. Though you may pay more for the proper stuff it will last longer, so proving more economical in the long run. *See also 242.*

Safe Driving

The Car

253 When choosing a car, look carefully at the interior design. For example, switches which stand proud of the dashboard are more dangerous in the event of an accident than those which are flush with the dashboard.

254 Look for a car with a thickly padded steering wheel, because this will offer greater accident protection than a simple spoked wheel.

255 Cars with a driver's seat which is adjustable for height and angle are much safer because you can achieve the best driving position for you, so enhancing your control, comfort and concentration – all vital for safe driving.

256 Most modern cars have height-adjustable front seat belts. Check that yours is set comfortably for you, especially if you share your driving with a partner of a different height or build. Incorrectly adjusted seat belts can cause neck injuries if you have to stop quickly, and could even fail to hold you in place properly during an accident. If your car doesn't have height-adjustable seat belts, a cushion on the seat is the safest alternative.

See also 19.

Your Driving

257 The first rule of safe driving is that both you and your car need to be in tip-top condition. So try to make sure that you are not tired when you get behind the wheel, and before you set off carry out the regular checks detailed in Chapter 4.

258 The real secret of safe and controlled driving is to drive smoothly, letting the car flow around corners and avoiding sudden braking or acceleration. This is especially important on corners or uneven road surfaces, because here the car can become unbalanced and you could lose control.

259 Be aware of your car's blind spots, especially when pulling out at junctions or when joining motorways or highways from a slip road.

260 When approaching a junction or roundabout, keep your eyes on the car in front of you rather than on the ones coming along – this situation is the most common cause of rear-end bumps. Once the car in front has pulled away cleanly, then is the time to look to right or left – never before.

261 Hold the steering wheel with both hands at all times, with your hands at two o'clock and ten o'clock.

262 When turning, always feed the steering wheel through your hands, never cross your hands or arms. If you do cross them you'll have very little control if the car goes into a skid.

263 When you are cornering, never brake hard. If you do you upset the balance of the car and cause it to swerve out of control, especially on wet or greasy road surfaces.

264 If you have a front wheel drive car, gently keep the power on as you corner because this has the effect of pulling the car cleanly through the corner.

265 If you are going into a corner in a front wheel drive car and you suddenly realize you are going too fast, don't panic. Come off the accelerator for a second and then smoothly apply power again. The more you accelerate the tighter the wheels will turn in, so pulling you round the corner.

266 If you drive a rear wheel drive car and the back end starts to slide when cornering, gently lift off the throttle pedal and the back end of the car should come back into line.

267 Don't brake heavily if the back end starts to break away, because this will allow the slide to continue.

268 An easy way to ensure you are far enough back from the vehicle in front is to say: 'Only a fool breaks the two-second rule' as the car in front passes, say, a lamp-post. If you can comfortably say the phrase before your car passes the same spot then you are far enough back to be able to stop in an emergency.

269 When driving on winding country roads, look ahead as far as possible. For instance, look across fields to pick up the road where it comes into view and reveals oncoming vehicles which may reach you in a minute or two. Then, if you come round a corner and find a broken-down vehicle or a herd of cows you should already have a fair idea if another vehicle is approaching, and be able to respond appropriately.

270 Beware of what's called 'dead ground' when driving on ordinary two-lane roads. This is where the road dips down out of sight. You may think you can see everything ahead, and that it's safe to overtake the vehicle in front, but any dead ground ahead could hide an oncoming vehicle which may suddenly pop up right in front of you.

271 Before overtaking on a two-lane road, look on both sides for any side roads or entrances to fields. If there are any, try and wait – otherwise another car or an agricultural vehicle could suddenly turn out of a field or road and drive straight into you while you are overtaking.

272 When overtaking, briefly flash your headlights at the car in front as you pull out. This is a legal requirement in some countries and its value cannot be underestimated – if the driver in front has not already seen you it should let him know you are coming past, and so it's less likely he will suddenly decide to turn into a side road as you overtake him.

273 If you're turning into a side street on the opposite side of the road, and you have to wait for oncoming traffic to pass, make sure your front wheels are pointing straight ahead. Then, if a car coming up behind you doesn't stop in time and hits you, you'll only be pushed ahead. But if your wheels are turned towards the side street you will be shunted straight into oncoming traffic – a common cause of road fatalities.

274 If you have to make an emergency stop and the wheels lock, you've effectively lost control of the car. To avoid this, at the first signs of the wheels locking take your foot off the brake pedal and then put it quickly back on again. Repeat until the car stops. You may need to do this extremely quickly if an emergency happens, so it makes sense to practise – it could save your life, and the lives of those around you.

275 Before you start to reverse you must be absolutely sure what is behind your car. Is there a small child playing? If in doubt, always get out and look first.

276 When reversing to park alongside the kerb, the easiest way to make sure that you are tight up against it is to line up the section of kerb that you can see out of your rear window with the bottom centre of the window. As you reverse, keep the kerb as central as you can in your screen. Then, when you come to a stop, you will be close up against the kerb.

277 If you have trouble judging distances, especially when reversing, or if you drive a vehicle which is high off the ground and therefore has limited rear vision, consider buying a distance bleeper which can be easily fitted to your rear bumper. The closer you get to any object behind, the more frequent are the bleeps. Such systems are not expensive and can save lives, especially those of small children who might be concealed behind your vehicle.

278 It's not a good idea to retune your car radio when driving. This is one of the most common causes of accidents, especially in towns and on motorways. (For the same reason, nor should you use most car phones while driving; *but see 346*.) Some radio systems, such as the Philips system which is fitted in certain French cars, are steering column-mounted and therefore better. They can be operated without you having to take your eyes off the road or your hands off the steering wheel.

○ *Eyesight*

279 As a general safety rule, have your eyes checked at least once every year – twice a year if you are over 60. Road safety experts say that about 50 per cent of drivers have some form of defective eyesight, which can be a serious contributory factor to road accidents.

280 If you wear glasses with light-reactive lenses be especially careful when driving from direct sunlight into tunnels. The lenses rarely have enough time to react to the sudden change and this means you can end up going into the tunnel totally blind.

281 Be very careful when driving at dusk, which is one of the most dangerous times of the day for drivers. In the dead of night there is often better overall visibility than at dusk when contours are vague and softened, which allows cars and people to blend into their surroundings all too easily and not be noticed.

282 At night, poor eyesight is especially dangerous. Check that you don't suffer from night blindness, which means that your sight is severely impaired during night driving.

○ *Night Driving*

283 If you are driving alone at night don't have the heater on too high. It is easy to fall asleep at the wheel if you get too comfortable.

284 Again if you're driving alone at night, switch on the radio and open a window. This is especially important if you are on a motorway or highway, where the repetitiveness of the surroundings can make you drop off to sleep.

285 If your car has no reversing lights and you need to reverse at night where there are no street lamps, put your hazard flashers on. These will supply enough light for you to see what is behind.

286 When driving at night, don't look into the lights of vehicles coming towards you, and always keep an eye out for cyclists, especially in town where the many different light sources can cause confusion.

○ *Long-distance Driving*

287 If driving a long distance, don't go for longer than three hours at one stretch – usually around 150 miles (240 km). After that your concentration and reactions are significantly and often dangerously dulled.

288 When you stop for a rest on a long journey, get out of the car and walk around. Also, if possible, have a drink – preferably of water or fruit juice – because dehydration can be a major problem when you're driving long distances.

○ *Alcohol*

289 Don't drive early in the morning if you've drunk a lot of alcohol the night before, because you may still be over the legal limit. It can take 12 hours for the alcohol in your bloodstream to drop below the legal permitted level for driving in most countries.

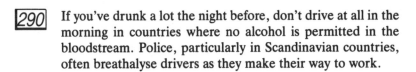

290 If you've drunk a lot the night before, don't drive at all in the morning in countries where no alcohol is permitted in the bloodstream. Police, particularly in Scandinavian countries, often breathalyse drivers as they make their way to work.

Bad Weather Driving

291 If you've been driving in fog, always check the following day that you haven't left your high-intensity rear fog-lamps on – in normal conditions their glare can temporarily blind following drivers.

292 Take extra care when driving on rain-sodden roads because above 50 mph (80 kph) there will be a film of water between each of your car's tyres and the road surface. This increases the risk of aqua-planing – the car literally floats on the road. If your car begins to aquaplane you will know, because the steering will suddenly become over-light. Try not to panic, don't brake or accelerate, but just keep the steering wheel in the same position. In most cases the small drop in speed will be sufficient for the car to regain its footing within seconds.

293 If you're driving a long distance in wet weather or in fog or mist, you should stop more often than usual – drive a maximum of 100 miles (160 km) between stops. Such driving is terribly tiring, and more concentration is demanded.

294 Every time you stop for a break when you're driving in the wet, clean your headlamps. It takes only 15–20 minutes' driving on a motorway or highway before they become coated in dirt, which can cut the light output by 30 per cent or more.

295 If you are travelling at high speeds in the rain and your car begins to aqua-plane sideways, threatening to go off the road, steer slightly into the slide and accelerate. With luck this will push the car back down on to the road.

296 Try not to brake on snow or ice because, if you do, you upset the balance of the car. Once the wheels lock you have lost control of the vehicle. If you do brake on ice or snow and the wheels lock, force yourself to step off the brake. The car will then once again be under control, allowing you to steer and accelerate.

297 As a general rule, while driving on snow or ice steer *into* any skid you find yourself in. This will slow the car, and when you gently accelerate it will get back on a straight line. But remember to steer *gently* into the skid – otherwise you'll find you've over-corrected the steering and the car will pendulum in the opposite direction.

298 If the back end of a rear wheel drive car begins to slew sideways on snow or ice, accelerate gently and steer into the slide. This should bring the back end neatly back on line.

299 As long as you keep your foot well clear of the brake when driving on ice and snow, and don't panic, the steering will still be operating fairly efficiently, so you should be able to steer around most obstacles.

300 If there is nothing you can do to avoid an object which you are hurtling towards on a wintry road, try driving your two side wheels off the slippery surface and on to the softer snow often found at the edge of the road. This can act as a brake, stopping the car as the snow bunches up under the wheels.

301 If you are driving in winter and suddenly there is silence from your tyres it means you've hit black ice. Don't panic – as long as the ice is on a straight stretch of road and you do nothing there is no reason why the car should slide. Remember, in any case, that black ice usually comes in patches no more than a few feet long, so your car should soon be back on to a non-icy road surface.

302 If the car does begin to slide on black ice – for example if you hit it while cornering – then don't brake, but try steering ever so slightly into the skid. This should be enough to right the car.

303 If you get your wheels stuck in deep snow don't try hard acceleration to get back out – all that happens is that the wheels dig themselves in even deeper.

304 If you do get stuck in deep snow, choose the highest possible gear without stalling the engine – usually second on a manual car, second or third on an automatic – and then accelerate very, very gently. If the wheels are still stuck, try reversing gently and then moving forwards gently. If the wheels seem well and truly dug in, wedge something under the wheels that they can grip against – an old blanket or other cloth, tree twigs and branches, sand or gravel, or a plank of wood.

305 Another way of getting the wheels free is to let almost all of the air out of the tyres which are stuck. This allows more tyre surface to come into contact with the road, so providing that much more grip.

306 If you drive a lot in snowy conditions make sure you always carry a tyre foot-pump in your car. It will be invaluable if you have just had to carry out the tip suggested above.

307 In countries with hard winters it also makes sense to carry a set of snow chains in the car. The best are those which simply wrap round the tyre – many of them have been designed to slip on to the tyre when the wheel is on the car.

308 Studded tyres can be useful in truly severe snow conditions, though they may have to be bolted on. They will also have to be taken off when driving on cleared roads because they provide dangerously poor grip on a solid tarmac surface.

Car Security and Personal Safety

Making Your Car Secure

In most European countries, and across North America, a car will be stolen every few seconds, usually by the casual, opportunist thief. Take the steps outlined here and it may not be your car which is stolen.

309 With one in five cars left unlocked by their owners, or with their windows left open, the first advice must be to ensure that your car is always locked (*but see also 384*) and that the windows and sunroof are closed. Also remember that as many as 60 per cent of stolen cars are taken from outside their owners' homes.

310 If you come home and find another car blocking your driveway, view it with suspicion because this is a method often used by car thieves. Many owners leave their own car unlocked while they go and look for the owner of the vehicle blocking their drive, and it's then that the car may be stolen. Alternatively, if you cannot find the driver you may eventually leave your car out in the roadway, so making the thief's job easier. (It may also affect your insurance cover if you leave your car outside your house.)

311 Beware of thieves setting your alarm off by rocking your parked car in the middle of the night, and then hiding. If they do it several times you may believe it's a false alarm. You get so fed up with the noise that you turn the alarm off – whereupon they come back and steal the car.

312 Never leave a coat on show in your car because a thief will wonder if money or other valuables are in any of the pockets, and may well break in just to find out.

313 If you have only basic insurance cover for your car, it's wise to get items such as coats, cameras, sunglasses and so on covered under your household insurance. Otherwise, if they are stolen from your car they will not be covered.

314 When away from home, try to leave your car in attended car parks. A favourite place for thieves to strike is at unattended airport and rail station car parks where they know there is a good chance of cars being left for hours, if not all day or even several days.

315 If you have to leave your car at night, park in a busy street where anyone trying to break in will usually be noticed.

316 Always try to park under a street lamp at night – it provides a heightened level of security.

317 Get all your car's windows security-etched with either the registration number or chassis number of your car. When a potential car thief sees this he will think twice about stealing your car because, while he can alter the identity of the car easily enough by changing the registration plates, it is far too expensive to replace all the glass.

318 If possible, keep the fuel level reasonably low because this not only aids fuel economy but, when used together with a locking fuel filler cap, means the thief will not get far.

319 If you have a stereo sound system fitted make sure that it either has a security code, so that it can only be used by you, or that it is removable so that you can take it with you when you leave the car.

320 Never leave your car's documents in the vehicle because they will make it that much easier for a thief to sell the car on. For example, if you leave any form of registration document he could immediately get the car reregistered in another name so that a new buyer might well not be aware it was stolen.

321 If you park in a pay-as-you-leave car park, always take your ticket with you. If you don't, a thief can easily take the car out without being challenged by staff at the gate or barrier.

322 Never leave in the car either a spare key or a note of its serial number.

323 If you are going on holiday early in the morning don't be tempted to load your car with luggage the night before – this is a favourite for thieves.

324 When loading your car with luggage, don't leave the car unattended while you go into the house to fetch more items, because the opportunist thief will often snatch luggage.

325 When you return from holiday, even if it is very late at night and you feel extremely tired, unload your car to stop thieves from unloading it for you overnight.

326 In fuel filling stations, don't leave your keys in the ignition while you go to pay – a surprisingly large number of cars are stolen this way.

327 Be particularly careful round about Christmas because this is the time you are most likely to take some of your shopping back to the car, then leave it while you go to buy more. A thief will often just smash a window, reach inside and grab your goods, so lock them out of sight in the boot or trunk of the car.

○ *The Best Types of Security Device*

Security devices buy time. A potential thief is likely to go along to the next car if he finds yours has a device fitted, so the expense is worthwhile.

328 Pick a device which immobilizes the car: either a steering wheel lock, or a lock which goes around the gear lever or clutch. These types are inexpensive, and, though hardly the last word in security, their visual deterrent is often good enough to deter the casual thief.

329 However, don't depend purely on a visual deterrent if your car is very expensive. Steering lock arms and gear lever locks often have very cheap and weak locking mechanisms which can easily be broken by sheer brute force. On a quality car, only use such a system in conjunction with a comprehensive alarm system.

330 A good alarm system includes ultrasonic protection and engine immobilization. The former protects the doors against forced entry – an alarm will sound – and senses air movement in the car, so nobody can climb through a smashed window without the alarm going off.

331 If you have fitted a simple trembler alarm which is activated when the car is moved or rocked – for example, when someone is trying to smash their way in, don't park on a busy road. If a large truck or bus thunders by, the shock waves may be enough to set the alarm off.

332 All alarm systems have a sensitivity switch, but make sure you don't turn it down too far or the alarm may not work at all when someone tries to break in.

333 If you have an ultrasonic alarm, remember to close the car's interior air vents when you park it and to activate the security system. Otherwise a passing vehicle may force air through the vents and into the car, where the air disturbance is often sufficient to set the alarm off.

334 Remember that any alarm system which is switched on by a hand-held remote control unit is only as good as the battery inside. Change the battery about every six months, or you may find you cannot deactivate the alarm to get into your own car!

335 Beware of the very simple alarm systems which use the car's horn to warn of a break-in. As the horn is always nearest the outside of the car – usually just behind the engine grille – it is easy for a criminal to reach in and snip the wires, thus killing the alarm.

336 Get a professional to fit your alarm. While this will make your alarm system cost more than if you fit it yourself, because most of them have to be carefully fitted into the electrical circuits it's worth having the job carried out by a specialist to make sure it's done right.

337 Drivers of convertible cars should not fit an ultrasonic alarm because the soft roofs of convertibles move, disturbing the air-flow inside the car and setting off false alarms.

338 If you have a convertible car insist that a microwave alarm is fitted. Microwaves are not disturbed by air-flow but only by a solid object passing through them, and they can be directed much more specifically than an ultrasonic system. This means that, even if the roof of your car is left down, the microwave system will still set the alarm off if anyone reaches inside.

339 Make sure that the alarm system you choose has a separate circuit to bypass your car's indicator direction signals. Some don't, and thieves who know this can disarm your car alarm in around two seconds.

340 Look for a car alarm which has a panic facility. If you are attacked when in your car, or even walking towards it, pressing the infra-red control device and therefore making the alarm sound will deter many potential attackers.

What to Do if Your Car Is Stolen

341 First check that you haven't parked your car somewhere else. This is not as silly as it sounds, for police estimate that around 10 per cent of cars reported stolen have simply been left elsewhere by their drivers!

342 If your car really has been stolen, call the police straightaway. Give them the exact location where the car was, a description of the vehicle, its registration number, and details of anything which you had in the car. This last point may help the police to establish quickly that the car is yours if they find it.

343 Once 24 hours has gone by since you reported the theft, get in touch with your insurance company. Different rules apply in different countries, but as a rule of thumb if your car has not been recovered within seven days – or is recovered but is so badly damaged that it is a complete write-off – you can then begin the procedure to claim on your insurance.

Safety in Cars

Unfortunately, it is an increasing fact of life that women are more at risk from harassment when driving than men are. These simple steps should ensure that you stay safer. There are also hints and tips to make sure that your children travel in the safest possible way.

344 A really good safety aid is the mobile phone, but make sure that you fully charge the batteries every day – otherwise the phone may not work properly when you need it most.

345 The best types of mobile phones are those which are compact enough to fit into a pocket or handbag but can also be slotted into a special power holster in the car. When used in the car such a system significantly increases the phone's power and therefore its range.

346 Look for a hands-free car phone-kit (this is a legal requirement in some countries) because then you can talk as you drive, without having to take your hands off the steering wheel.

347 Always carry an up-to-date map so that you can check where you are if you happen to get lost. It will mean that you shouldn't have to ask a stranger for directions.

348 If you see a woman hitch-hiking by herself, don't assume it will be safe to pick her up. She may have a male accomplice hiding nearby.

349 If someone seems to need help, don't stop. Drive on until you can call the police or breakdown services for assistance.

350 If another driver signals to you that something is wrong with your car, don't stop, but slow down and wait until you can safely stop to get out and have a look. Increasingly, this ploy is used by car-jackers to get you to stop.

351 It's sensible to drive with your doors locked, especially when driving at night in city streets, or even at slow speeds in town during the day.

352 Most cars with central door locking can be locked from inside and then opened normally from inside. However, it is worth remembering that if you have an accident it will be harder for rescuers to get you out of the car.

353 If your car has central locking, check with the car dealer that it has a safety device built in which allows the door locks to pop back up if the car is involved in a serious accident. In some countries this device is a legal requirement, and it responds to a severe blow to the body of the car.

354 When parking, think carefully about where you are leaving your car. To avoid harassment, try to park in well-lit streets, near to houses, and as close to your final destination as possible.

355 If you are using a multi-storey car park try and find a space close to the exit, at ground level or near to it, and away from any large pillars where somebody might hide. When you come back to your car have your keys out and ready so that you can get in quickly.

356 If you believe someone is following you when driving, drive to the nearest police station.

357 If one of the worst scenarios happens, and someone swerves their car across yours, forcing you to stop, don't panic. Wait until they get out of their car, then put yours in reverse and drive backwards until you can swing your car around and head off in the opposite direction. But don't drive backwards too fast because it is all too easy to burn the clutch out on a manual car, or cause the gearbox to seize on an automatic. That would make you stranded.

358 If someone tries to get into your car in a busy city street, sound your horn and don't stop until someone comes to your aid. The attacker will usually run off.

See also 434.

○ *Safety on the Motorway or Highway*

359 If you break down on the motorway, remember that in most countries emergency phones are no more than a mile apart (1.6 km), so try and coast your car along to the next one before stopping.

360 If you are a woman using the emergency phone make sure to mention you are a lone female, because this will give you priority and ensure that someone gets to you quickly.

361 When making such a call, stand behind the phone and look towards oncoming traffic. This way you will see if anyone is coming towards you and it will be less obvious to passing motorists that you are a woman alone.

362 When you return to your car it's safest, in many respects, to sit up on the embankment, simply because cars can get hit by other vehicles when they are sitting on the hard shoulders of motorways, often with fatal consequences.

363 If you do sit on the embankment, lock all your car's doors except for the passenger door. Then if someone does appear to be approaching, and he's not from one of the emergency services, you can quickly get back into your car and lock yourself in.

364 Another safety point about sitting in the passenger seat is that it looks as though you are accompanied and that your partner has gone off to make the rescue call.

365 If someone does approach, wind your window down a fraction – only sufficient to hold a conversation.

366 Make sure that anyone who approaches and says he is from the emergency or breakdown services has your name.

367 If a stranger stops and offers to help, ask him to call the emergency services for you but don't accept any other form of assistance.

368 Buy an emergency sign that says 'PLEASE CALL POLICE' in bold letters. If you break down in a place where there isn't a phone, or you cannot get out to obtain help, stick this sign in your back window and a passing motorist should soon call for help for you.

○ *Pregnant Women*

369 If you drive when pregnant you must still wear a seat belt. Make sure that the belts cross your body above and below your stomach.

370 If you feel uncomfortable driving while pregnant, then it's important that you don't. If you're not comfortable it means you cannot concentrate properly on driving and this is not good either for you or for your unborn child.

See also 255.

○ *Children in Cars*

371 Never let your baby travel on anyone's lap in the front of the car. In the event of a serious accident the adult will crash forwards and crush the baby, even if a seat belt is being worn.

372 If you are a mother travelling alone with your young baby, pick one of the special safety cots which straps into the car using the car's own front seat belt, and which has the baby facing the car's seat back. This excellent system allows the baby to see you, it provides the best protection in the event of a serious accident, and it means you can look at the baby without having to turn around and take your eyes off the road.

373 Always firmly strap young children, and especially babies, into the car in specially designed safety seats. If you don't, in the event of an accident they will be shot forwards with the speed of a bullet.

374 When choosing a child seat, check it is compatible with your car by ensuring that your car's seat belt buckles do not foul on the child seat frame, and that the car's seat belt sockets are correctly positioned when the child seat is placed on the car's seat. Check also that the car has sufficient seat belt length to keep the child in comfortably.

375 When buying a child seat for the back seats, make sure that you pick the right size. There is no point buying a bigger seat than you need at the time because the child will not be safe strapped in a seat which is too big. Child seats are designed for children up to the age of thirteen. Every six months, especially when a baby is very young and growing quickly, check that he or she still fits comfortably, and therefore safely, into the seat.

376 As a rule, children under 10 should not sit in the front of a car because even if they are strapped in the belts may not fit adequately, simply because they have been designed for fully grown adults. If you have to brake suddenly, the child may dive under the belts and be badly injured. In many countries children are banned by law from the front passenger seat.

377 In most countries it is now a legal requirement to wear a seat belt in the back of a car, as well as in the front. This advice is especially important for children, because they get thrown about more easily in the event of a serious accident.

378 Make sure that you engage the child locks on all rear doors. These locks are fitted by law on every car with rear doors and are switched on and off by a small lever or pin inside the door.

379 On all cars with all-round electric windows you can disengage the rear windows by pushing a button or switch near the driver. If you have children in the car switch the rear windows off so that they cannot suddenly get them to go down and clamber out, or stick their arms or head out.

380 When buying a car with electric windows check that it has a safety cut-off device, and that it works. The theory is that if the window is going up and a child has his arm or head in the way of the window it will stop going up when it touches the child. Some cars still do not have such safety devices, and a number of children worldwide have been killed by windows which would not stop going up and so choked them to death.

○ *Animals in Cars*

381 Never let a small dog travel on the back shelf. If you hit another car it will hurtle forward like a bullet, injuring passengers and probably killing itself.

382 If you travel with a dog a dog guard should always be fitted to stop the animal getting into the front of the car, but if you buy an estate car or station wagon look for the ones which have tie hooks in the cargo area. Your dog's lead can be tied to one of these if the animal is especially excitable when he's in the car.

383 If you want your cat to travel with you it's best to put it in a special cat basket. Don't let it run around loose because, although it may happily travel in the car, it could be frightened by a dog outside and then start to run around, getting under the pedals, or jump on to your shoulders and cause you to swerve.

384 If you have to leave your pets in the car for a short while make sure that there are plenty of windows open, and try and park in a shady spot, especially in hot weather. A dog cannot sweat like human beings and so its body temperature can rise rapidly and sometimes fatally.

385 Use a special non-drip water bottle clipped to the dog guard when transporting your pets for any distance, because animals generally dehydrate far more quickly than humans.

Accidents and Breakdowns

386 It's a good idea to make sure that your insurance cover is always up-to-date, and that all relevant facts, such as a driving conviction or health problem, have been given to the insurance company. If you don't, you could find the policy is null and void when an accident happens.

387 It's important to keep your car in good mechanical condition, and always to ensure that the tyres have at least the minimum legal tread depth, because if you have an accident and your car is not legally roadworthy then your insurance policy may be invalid.

388 Always carry a pen and paper in your car, because if you are unfortunate enough to have an accident you will have to record all the details.

What to Do After an Accident

389 After an accident, above all keep calm. Even if you know it was the other driver's fault, try and keep your temper – because frayed tempers never help.

390 It's wise never to admit liability, even if you know it was your fault. The reason is that you might find after the event that the other driver was under the influence of alcohol, for example, or driving without insurance, or otherwise illegally, and this could have a major effect on the outcome of any subsequent legal case. If you do admit it was your fault the driver has a much stronger case, and even if he was not driving totally legally he could still successfully win damages from you.

391 Find out if anyone is injured and attend to them first before you do anything else. Call for an ambulance and remember that if someone is injured, even if it only seems to be a graze, it is a legal requirement in all countries to call the police.

392 Don't remove an injured person from the car, unless they are in further danger by being left there. Just try and make them as comfortable as possible and ensure they are kept warm. Don't give them anything to eat and drink in case they have internal injuries.

393 If the vehicles are in a dangerous position – blocking the road, or stopped on a dangerous bend or junction – try and move them, but not before taking careful note of their exact positions.

394 Make sure that no one in the immediate area is smoking, just in case there is a fuel spillage.

395 If no one has been injured there is no need to call the police. However, if a dog has caused the accident and it has been killed, in most countries the police should be notified, though this does not have to be done at the time of the accident. If a cat, hedgehog, rabbit or raccoon has been killed the police do not need to be informed.

396 It's a good idea to sketch out a diagram of the accident, showing where the vehicles started and where they ended up, and indicating distances. Include anything that you feel may have contributed to the accident, such as a parked vehicle or road works. And finally jot down some notes about the accident and how you perceived it. Mention time of day, weather and road conditions (for example, was the surface wet, or icy, or poorly maintained) and the speed of the vehicles involved – all of these can be important contributory factors to an accident.

397 If there are any witnesses to the accident make sure you get their names and addresses before they drive away. This is crucial in case the other driver or drivers dispute your version of events leading up to the accident.

398 Always take down the names of other drivers or passengers involved in the accident, and make a note of the registration numbers of all vehicles. Exchange insurance details with other drivers.

399 Contact your insurance company within 24 hours – in most countries it's a legal requirement that you do so within this time – and ask for a claim form. Fill it in straightaway, while the accident is still fresh in your mind.

400 If your car needs to be repaired, it is wise to get at least two estimates: firstly, because most insurance companies will demand two, and secondly, because it will give you a truer idea of the repair costs.

401 Remember that, even if you have got estimates for repair work on your car, it cannot go ahead until you have written authorization from your insurance company.

Basic Breakdown Diagnosis

How to find out what is wrong if your car will not start, or begins to break down.

402 This may seem obvious, but if your car is hard to start check there is fuel in the tank! Each year in the UK alone, around 70,000 drivers run out of fuel and have to be rescued.

403 The safest and most legal spare fuel cans are those which have a foil safety mesh inside. This stops fuel surging about when the car is being driven, and therefore prevents the build-up of excessive pressure inside the can.

404 Always make sure that the spare petrol can is placed in the boot (trunk) of the car so that dangerous petrol fumes are kept at bay. However, if you have an early Austin Mini don't put a fuel can in the boot because this is where the battery is placed. A battery fault could cause a spark, which might ignite any fumes that had escaped from the petrol can.

Electrical Problems

405 Turn the key and nothing happens at all? It's an electrical fault. The most common is a flat battery (*see 409–18*) but if the lights still work, and are still bright, it will be an electrical ignition problem. In this case try turning the key a few times – the cause could be a bad connection which may work after a few tries.

406 If the engine turns over but will not fire fully, it's usually a fuel problem. Try rocking the car gently, because if it's a fuel blockage this can sometimes cure it.

407 If the car begins to stutter and misfire this also could be due to insufficient fuel getting through. However it could also be an electrical problem, such as the engine's alternator beginning to fail. Keep the car going – if you stop, the engine will almost certainly cut out – and almost certainly not start again. Get yourself to a service bay.

Clutch

408 If you drive a manually geared car and the engine seems to race on after you've just changed up a gear, then the clutch is badly worn and may fail within 40 or 50 miles (80 km). Get the car into a service bay as soon as possible, and on the way there try to use the clutch as little as possible.

Flat Batteries and How to Cure Them

409 Make sure you never leave your headlights or radio on because this will soon cause a flat battery, one of the most common causes of car breakdown across the world.

410 When using jump-leads to get a flat battery going, make sure that one of the leads goes from the positive terminal on the good battery to the positive on the dead battery. The other, of course, should go negative to negative.

411 Make sure that there are no flammable liquids anywhere near the car when connecting jump-leads, because there can be a sudden cluster of sparks as the terminals are connected up.

412 Be very careful not to touch the end of one connected cable to the end of the other connected cable, as this can cause the donor battery suddenly to explode, spewing acid all over the place. Similarly, don't allow the 'live' end to touch any other part of the car other than the battery terminal, as this can cause a short-circuit which could damage the donor battery, or even the electrical system of either car. In some cases this can also cause the battery to explode.

413 Start the car that has the good battery, and then try starting the car that has the flat battery. In some cases it may not work the first time, so have about three or four goes. If it still doesn't start, the problem may be elsewhere.

414 If you don't have any jump-leads, or there is no other car to hitch them up to, try to push-start the car by getting someone to push it while you steer. Once the car is travelling at around 8 mph/13 kph (jogging speed), put it into gear and then slowly let the clutch come up. The car should start.

415 Never be tempted to try and bump-start the car yourself if it is on a slight gradient, because you may have to push the car while steering through the open door. All too often in such situations the car will pick up speed so quickly that it's impossible for you to jump back in fast enough!

416 Never try to bump-start or tow-start a car fitted with a catalytic convertor. This method will damage the catalytic unit so badly that it will need replacing.

417 It's not possible to bump-start an automatic geared car, so in this situation it's especially important to carry jump-leads.

418 If you have left the lights on and the battery has gone flat, but you have now been able to restart the car, run it for 15–25 miles to allow the battery to recharge properly. If you don't, you may be stranded again as soon as you switch the engine off.

○ *Fanbelt*

419 If the fanbelt snaps, a good emergency repair can be made with a pair of women's tights. Simply loop them around the two fly wheels in the engine and tie them as tightly as possible. This temporary repair should get you home.

○ *Changing a Wheel Quickly, Safely and Cleanly*

420 Tyres and wheels are always really dirty, so keep in the car a pair of old kitchen gloves which you can slip on if you have to change a wheel. This will save you arriving at your destination with grubby hands.

421 Always carry a can of aerosol-based tyre sealant. This can provide a very quick and efficient temporary repair to a tyre which has a small, slow puncture, perhaps as a result of driving over a little nail or a thorn. Simply screw the aerosol's adaptor to your tyre's valve and press the aerosol's trigger to fill the tyre with air and a special sealant. Immediately drive 15–25 miles (25–40 km) for the sealant to spread right around the inside of the tyre.

422 If the puncture is a large hole then you will have to fit the spare wheel which must be carried by law, and whose tyre must have the minimum legal tread depth.

423 To make sure that the car is not damaged if it falls off the jack, and that you are not trapped underneath, remove the spare wheel from its housing and place it flat just under the side of the car. Then, if the car tips off the jack, the spare wheel will form a cushion between it and the ground.

424 If the ground is soft, place a plank of wood (always carry a small plank in the car boot) down first and then put the jack on top. This way the jack will not sink down into the ground as you jack the car up.

425 Don't start jacking the car up until you have consulted the car's handbook and found where the jacking points are. There will normally be one on either side of the car at the front and the rear, and it's imperative that you only use the jack at these places because they are constructed of strengthened steel specially built to take the car's weight. If you jack the car elsewhere along its underside the jack could make a hole in the belly of the car, and the car could crash back down on to the ground.

426 Jack up the car until the wheel is just about to lift off the ground. Then use the wheelbrace to loosen all the bolts until you can move them with your fingers. Now jack the car several inches or centimetres further, so there's sufficient room to put the spare wheel on once you've removed the wheel with the punctured tyre.

427 In order to avoid straining your back, place the wheelbrace on one of the wheel nuts and then try pushing it down with your foot. If the nuts are too tight, try standing on the wheelbrace, first making sure it is firmly attached to the nut.

428 When removing the old wheel, push your foot, or a hand, against the bottom edge of the punctured tyre so that it keeps flat against the wheel. Then remove the bottom bolts first.

429 Wheels are heavy, so check where the bolt holes are and line them up before you pick the new wheel up. Then it can easily be slid straight on to the bolts.

430 Tighten the nuts by hand before you let the wheel down on to the ground. After you have let the wheel down, always tighten the nuts with the wheelbrace as much as possible.

431 Replace the old tyre as soon as possible – many people forget to do so, and are then stranded if they have another puncture. Remember, also, that it's illegal to carry a spare which is not fully inflated.

What to Do if You Break Down While Driving

432 Pull as far over to the side of the road as possible, put your hazard warning lights on and place your warning triangle (you are obliged to carry one by law in many countries, especially in Europe), about 100 feet (35 metres) behind the car. On motorways, highways and autoroutes the triangle should be a minimum of 300 feet (100 metres) behind the car.

433 Make sure that you always carry a torch, a waterproof coat, some money and a phone card. These may be really useful if you break down.

434 If you belong to a breakdown organization get in touch with them, because they will help you get back on the road as soon as possible and at minimum cost.

435 Even if you are not a member of a breakdown organization it often makes sense to get in touch with them and tell them you will become a member if they come and rescue you. Across the world, some breakdown groups will come to your aid in these circumstances. In the UK, National Breakdown will rescue non-members, though they charge a small call-out fee as well as charging for any new parts. In the USA and Canada you can usually be rescued for a small fee, even if you are not a member.

436 If you have called a breakdown organization, make sure that when the rescue vehicle arrives it is from the company you have called. If it isn't, refuse their offer of help because private firms may well charge you a small fortune.

437 Never get in a car with a stranger, or try and hitch a lift.

438 If you haven't got a car phone, before you set off to call the breakdown company make sure you have your membership details with you as well as a note of your car's registration number, and that you are able to tell them just where you have broken down.

439 Make sure you can give a rough idea of what you believe the problem to be – for example, whether you think it is an electrical fault or a mechanical one. The trained telephonists will be able to get a fair idea of the problem when they talk to you.

440 If you have to set off for a phone and it's late afternoon or early evening, take your torch because darkness will probably close in before you get back to your car.

441 If you have children with you, take them with you, but pets should be left in the car with a couple of windows slightly open. Don't worry, no one can steal your car – it has broken down!

See also Chapter 7.

The Motorist and the Law

Laws vary from country to country, of course, but here are some tips to help you stay on the right side of the law wherever you're driving.

442 If a police officer in uniform requests you to stop you should do so as soon as possible, because failure to stop is an offence in itself. This general rule applies in all countries.

443 If you are asked to stop by someone claiming to be a police officer but who is not in uniform and who is not in a clearly marked police car, then you should be suspicious. In most countries it is not a legal requirement to stop under such circumstances.

444 If you live in a built-up area it may be illegal to wash your car in the street. This applies in many British cities, and in Germany you are not allowed to wash your car except in a proper car-wash.

445 All windows and mirrors should be kept clean. If they aren't, police officers can report you and in some countries you may have to pay an on-the-spot fine.

446 You must always have at least two rear view mirrors, and in many countries, especially in Europe, at least one of these mirrors has to be mounted on the outside of the vehicle.

447 Don't sound your horn if your car is stationary – this is an offence in most countries. The obvious exception is if you are warning another driver that you are parked there – perhaps they are rolling their vehicle back into yours, for example.

448 In most metropolitan areas – usually classified as a street where the road lights are less than 200 yards/metres apart – it is an offence to sound your horn between 11.30 p.m. and 7 a.m. This time span varies from country to country, but essentially you should not use your car's horn during the night – unless, of course, it's for an emergency.

449 Try not to reverse for too great a distance – not that you will usually have to – because most countries view excessive reversing as an offence since it can endanger pedestrians and other road users.

450 It's worth ensuring that your vehicle's exhaust system is not corroded or holed, because excessive noise is an offence.

451 Don't overload your car, or have pets scampering around inside. All countries have laws about driving while not in a position to have control, and this can include vision through your rear view mirror being obscured by a mountain of luggage or a dog sitting on your lap – it happens!

452 Don't step out on to a pedestrian crossing in any mainland European country if a car is coming because – unlike in the UK – drivers do not have to stop even if the pedestrian is right in the middle of the crossing (though a French policeman once rather drily told me, 'But if you are hit it is the driver's fault'). This may be little compensation as you are fighting for life, so the best tip is don't try it.

453 Don't drink and drive. Although there are sometimes differing legal limits for the amount of alcohol allowed in your bloodstream (depending on which country you are driving in), it simply is not worth risking. One in three of all drivers killed worldwide has been found to have been drinking alcohol.

454 Remember that in almost all countries it is a legal requirement that seat belts should be worn, and in most European countries this now applies to those travelling in the back seats, too. Failure to do so can result in legal action.

455 If you do end up in court for any alleged offence, it is important to be well prepared. Retain a legal representative, who will not only know and understand the law but will also have experience of working in the sometimes confusing arena of the courtroom.

456 If you believe you have been wrongly accused, seek legal advice to see if you are correct and marshal as much evidence as you can, including any witness statements and photographs of the scene if the legal action is as a result of an accident. *See also Chapter 8.*

Driving Abroad

For obvious reasons, 'abroad' means different things to different people. Here are some general points to note – consult a motoring guide for information on specific countries.

457 Read carefully the small print on any mechanical breakdown cover which you organize through a travel agent or a motoring organization. Make sure it includes cover to transport the car back home if it requires a major repair or if it is involved in a serious accident.

458 Check that you and your family will be covered for any medical problems which might occur when you are driving abroad. In some countries – across the European Community, for example – there are reciprocal health arrangements, usually at no cost, but in other countries you may need additional medical cover.

459 Before you go, decide how you are going to pay for fuel. This can be very important; for example, in Norway and Finland most filling stations only accept either cash or local bank cards – you could find that cards such as Visa, Mastercard and Amex are virtually unacceptable for fuel.

460 If travelling in eastern European countries, check before you go about money, because some countries – Russia, for example – still give tokens and vouchers which are exchanged for fuel. You have to order and pay for them before you enter the country, rather than paying cash or using a credit card on the spot.

461 Although not a legal requirement in all countries (though it is in much of Europe) it makes sense to carry a warning triangle for use if you have broken down. In some countries it's a legal requirement to have two warning triangles – one to be placed in front of the vehicle, the other behind.

462 Carry a spare set of bulbs for your car. In some countries this is a legal requirement, but even if it isn't it makes sense because, if your car is not made in the country you are visiting, you may have difficulty getting replacements if a bulb blows.

463 Whenever you drive abroad take an international driving licence. Your local motoring organization can normally supply one. Although it is not a legal requirement in many countries today, it makes for a much easier life if you are stopped by the police and asked to produce your documents.

464 In the European Community there is no longer any need to carry an insurance Green Card. All you need are the vehicle's registration documents to prove that it belongs to you or your company.

465 Your car could be confiscated by foreign police if you cannot pay an on-the-spot fine, so make sure you know exactly what the national speed limits are – there is no defence in saying that you are a foreigner.

466 Before you set off abroad, check if you have to carry a bail bond – a legal document which shows that if you are arrested for a serious driving offence any bail or damages will be paid for by your insurance company. This is a particular requirement of Spain.

467 Obviously it's not sensible to drink and drive, but particular care needs to be taken when driving abroad because different countries – and in the USA, different States – have different permitted levels of alcohol when driving, and differing penalties for those who break the law.

468 Don't carry a spare can of petrol in your car if driving in Greece, San Marino or Italy, because it is illegal.

469 Don't pick up hitch-hikers when driving abroad, but especially in Austria. In the areas of Bürgenland, Styria, Upper Austria and Vorarlberg it is illegal for persons under the age of 16 to hitch, so if you pick someone up in any of these areas you could be an accessory to a crime!

470 Take extra care when driving in towns and cities in France and Denmark, where there is still a basic requirement that you have to give way to traffic coming from the right. This is incredibly confusing because if there is a solid white line across a side road on your right it means you have right of way. But . . . if there isn't a line, then traffic entering your road from the side road has right of way, and that can mean you have to stop, even on main roads.

471 In France take particular care when approaching roundabouts, because drivers coming on to them used to have right of way. Rather than make all roundabouts identical, French road planners have introduced an element of Russian roulette by retaining some roundabouts where priority is for those coming on, and building others where the rules are as in the rest of Europe. Where there is a sign saying *'Vous n'avez pas la priorité'* (or *'Cédez le passage'*) traffic already on the roundabout has priority, but if there is no such sign the traffic coming on to the roundabout has priority. Keep your fingers crossed that the sign has not blown down!

472 If you enter a tunnel anywhere in Italy or Switzerland, even one which is very well lit, remember that it is a legal requirement to switch your headlights on. Italian police in particular often wait in tunnels to catch those who do not follow the letter of the law.

473 In Norway, Sweden, Finland and Iceland make sure that your dipped headlights are always on, because it's a legal requirement even during daylight hours.

474 As a general rule, make sure that you do not drive only on side lights, no matter which country you are visiting, as it is usually an offence to drive at night on anything other than dipped headlights. One exception is Spain, where side lights are permitted as long as you are driving on well-lit urban roads.

475 If you are stopped by the police in any country other than your own and are told you've committed an offence and that you must pay an on-the-spot fine, make sure that the police officer gives you a proper official receipt.

476 It's a legal requirement in most countries to carry a first aid kit in your car. Make sure you buy or make up a kit which contains plenty of bandages, sticky plaster, basic medicines and antiseptic.

477 If you are driving in the USA or Canada and you find you are following a yellow school bus, remember that if it stops you are not allowed to overtake it, just in case children decide to cross in front of the bus. Also, even if you are driving towards the bus on the other side of the road, and it stops, you too must stop – again because children may decide to cross.

478 In a large number of US States, especially those in New England, it's possible to turn right on a red light, unless it says otherwise – a manoeuvre not generally permitted in Europe.

479 If you are driving in France and you see two wires across the road on motorways and main roads, slow down quickly because you are about to cross a speed trap. The police often place the wires under bridges, where the shadows partially hide them. Watch out!

480 Don't try to out-speed the police in Holland – their motorway officers drive 170 mph (270 kph) Porsche 911s.

481 If you want to use a car-wash in the USA, have a good look before you go in. Some US car-washes drag the car through by its wheels – unlike the European ones where brushes advance on the car. If you do go into one of these US car-washes, don't leave your handbrake on, and if you are driving an automatic car don't leave it in 'park' or the dragging mechanism will try to tear the car's wheels off!

Selling Your Car

Presentation

482 Get your car properly valeted inside and out before you put it up for sale, and you'll definitely recoup the cost. A car in good, clean condition can fetch up to 10 per cent more than a car which looks tatty and poorly cared for.

483 If your car has small stone chips on the bonnet – most cars suffer from this problem sooner or later – it may well be worth touching them up. Make sure that you get the exact colour, preferably buying a touch-up stick from your nearest franchised dealer.

484 In some cases it may not be worth touching up the stone chips. Why? Because some modern cars have plastic bonnets, which of course will not rust, so very small stone chips often look better left than poorly touched up.

485 If you do touch up the bodywork it's a good idea to polish over the area – once the paintwork has thoroughly dried and hardened, ideally after two to three days – with a paintwork cutting agent such as T-Cut. This will blend the touched up colour into the surrounding paintwork, which may well have slightly faded since you bought the car.

486 Make sure that all the lights are working, and all electrical items. If you have a couple of minor items on your car which need replacing – say the radio doesn't work, or one of the windscreen wipers is defective – get them replaced before you put the car up for sale. If you leave them it gives a buyer the chance to make you drop your price, and immediately gives him the advantage.

487 Make sure that all fluid levels – brakes, radiator, clutch – are fully topped up.

488 Fill up the fuel tank – it may seem a small point, but it can make a potential buyer happier.

489 Collect all the car's documents and organize them all in a smart wallet.

Selling Privately

490 For the best price, sell your car privately. You can get around 10 per cent more than if you sell to a dealer, because a dealer who buys from you will need to add his own 10–15 per cent mark-up before he puts your car up for sale in his dealership.

491 Don't keep the car for anybody unless they pay a deposit and say they will return soon, because those who don't pay a deposit often don't come back.

492 Be honest when selling – it can land you in trouble if you make excessive claims for your car which later turn out to be untrue.

493 Before putting your car up for sale, research its secondhand value and then ask a sensible price. If you pitch it too high you will almost certainly end up having to drop the price anyway.

494 Remember that if the buyer offers you a cheque you will have to wait several days for it to clear. Don't be tempted to let him have the car before it clears, even if he claims to live near you.

495 Always telephone the bank if the person who wants to buy your car offers a banker's draft or money order. This used to be a cast-iron way of paying for a car, but worldwide there has been a worrying increase in the number of banker's drafts being stolen and then fraudulently used. Tell the buyer you are going to call the bank to check the serial number. An honest buyer will not object to such a precaution – a dishonest one will.

496 Obvious point: don't let them go on a test drive by themselves!

Selling at Auction

497 Want to sell your car quickly? Then selling at auction could be the answer, but care is needed. Put your car in with a reserve price on it – this means it will not be sold if bidding does not reach this value.

498 You will be charged a fee when you put your car in for auction, so price it sensibly so that you are not throwing your money away.

499 Do your homework on the value of your car before putting it in for auction. You can most easily do this by visiting the auction house at least three times just before you put your own car in. Make a note of the prices that similar cars to yours are fetching, and watch how quickly they are selling.

500 You will usually sell for less at an auction than if you were selling privately because a trade buyer will have to put his mark-up – usually about 10 per cent – on the car before he resells it.

501 It is particularly important that your car looks in tip-top condition (bodywork, interior, underneath the car and in the engine compartment) because most auction buyers are from the trade and they will always choose a clean car as opposed to a dirty one. In addition, cars cannot be test driven at most auction sites, so clean looks and the mileage are the major factors on which a buyer makes his decision.

See also 52–6.

ALSO AVAILABLE FROM PIATKUS BOOKS

1001 Supersavers

Pamela Donald

Here are 1001 brilliant ideas – guaranteed to save you time and money around the home. Tried and tested by well-known writer and broadcaster Pamela Donald, *1001 Supersavers* contains loads of tips for everyone.

Sections include:

THE DIY BUFF	GREEN FINGERS
HOUSEHOLD HINTS	THE FAMILY PET
CHEF'S TIPS	KIDS' STUFF
CLOTHES CARE	ON THE MOVE
HEALTH MATTERS	BRIGHT IDEAS

ALSO AVAILABLE FROM PIATKUS BOOKS